# On Ovid's *Metamorphoses*

*Gareth Williams*

CORE KNOWLEDGE

CORE KNOWLEDGE

The Core Knowledge series takes its motivation from the goals, ideals, challenges, and pleasures of Columbia College's Core Curriculum. The aim is to capture the intellectual energy and the stimulus to creative thinking that is a fundamental ideal of such courses as Literature Humanities and Contemporary Civilization. In the spirit of Core teaching, the books are intended to reflect on what the featured works *can* be if approached from different or unusual vantage points; how they may inform modern experience, and how they are to be viewed not as sources of plain fact, certainty, and assured beliefs but as provocations to the imagination that help us to see differently, experimentally, and with a spirit of intellectual adventure.

EDITORIAL BOARD

# On
# Ovid's
# *Metamorphoses*

Gareth Williams

Columbia University Press / *New York*

Columbia University Press
*Publishers Since 1893*
New York   Chichester, West Sussex
cup.columbia.edu
Copyright © 2023 Columbia University Press

Library of Congress Cataloging-in-Publication Data
Names: Williams, Gareth D., author.
Title: On Ovid's Metamorphoses / Gareth Williams.
Other titles: Core knowledge (Columbia College (Columbia
University))
Description: New York : Columbia University Press, 2022. |
Series: Core knowledge | Includes bibliographical references
and index.
Identifiers: LCCN 2022027557 (print) | LCCN 2022027558 (ebook) |
ISBN 9780231200707 (hardcover) | ISBN 9780231200714
(trade paperback) | ISBN 9780231553759 (ebook)
Subjects: LCSH: Ovid, 43 B.C.–17 A.D. or 18 A.D. Metamorphoses. |
Ovid, 43 B.C.–17 A.D. or 18 A.D.—Themes, motives. | Change in
literature. | Metamorphosis in literature. | Fables, Latin—History and
criticism. | Latin poetry—History and criticism.
Classification: LCC PA6519.M9 W55 2022  (print) | LCC PA6519.
M9 (ebook) | DDC 873/.01—dc23/eng/20220726
LC record available at https://lccn.loc.gov/2022027557
LC ebook record available at https://lccn.loc.gov/2022027558

Cover design: Lisa Hamm
Cover image: Scala / Art Resource, NY

*In fond memory of Deborah Martinsen*

# Contents

# Preface

For many years, Ovid's *Metamorphoses* has regularly featured on the syllabus of Columbia College's fabled Literature Humanities course, which is standardly taken by all first-year students as a staple part of the Columbia Core Curriculum. This little book is designed to capture some of the energy and excitement that Ovid's poem tends to generate in the Core classroom, but also to explore some of the ways in which this centuries-old work speaks to a modern audience with a timeless human relevance and meaning. The *Metamorphoses* is far too complex, slippery, maddening, troubling, and enthralling for its essence to be easily captured or conveyed in words, least of all in the pages presented here. The aim is rather to explore some experimental angles of approach to the poem, to address some of the challenges that confront Ovid's newest audience in our fast-moving times, and to suggest why it speaks in compelling ways to a twenty-first-century readership.

On offer here is not so much an introduction to the *Metamorphoses* or a ministudy that is meant to prepare the interested reader for scaling this Eiger of an epic. Rather, this contribution is meant either as a brisk companion piece as you embark on your own reading of the poem or as a point of comparison (and disagreement!) after you have voyaged through Ovid's fifteen books. It is intended to provoke and challenge, but always with the premise that change is not just the main theme of the *Metamorphoses* but also its essential dynamic and point of relevance to Ovid's reader: here is a poem that ceaselessly focuses on the changefulness of human experience, on the unpredictability of shifting circumstances as our fortunes ebb and flow in life, and on the transformations encoded in our existence as we grow older, modify our viewpoints, adapt to changing times, or evolve out of our former selves.

The translation used in this book is David Raeburn's in the Penguin Classics series, with some occasional modifications. Published by Penguin Books in 2004, it has been standardly used when, in recent years, Ovid's *Metamorphoses* has been included in the Columbia College Literature Humanities syllabus. There is not much quotation from Ovid's Latin in this book, but when the text is cited, the edition followed is that of Richard J. Tarrant in the Oxford Classical Texts series (Oxford University Press, 2004). At many points in the chapters that follow, specialists in the field of Ovidian studies would recognize familiar ideas and the influence of well-known scholarly sources; nonetheless, various attempts at fresh interpretation are made along the way. The lack of footnotes is in keeping with the spirit of the Core Knowledge series, but suggestions for further reading are offered at the end of the book. The four main chapters offer snapshots of main thematic preoccupations in the *Metamorphoses*, but they do not provide what has already been very well supplied by accomplished scholars—namely, a much more comprehensive, systematic, and methodical treatment of the content and narrative strategies that Ovid deploys in this great poem.

I am grateful to Jeremy Dauber, Claudia Heilbrunn, Philip Kitcher, Elisabeth Ladenson, Carole Newlands, Lucy Nicholas, and Nadia Urbinati for many valuable insights, reactions, and points of advice that have helped this project beyond measure. Readers for Columbia University Press offered a wealth of suggestions for improvement, and I here gratefully acknowledge their many ideas and correctives that have shaped the final outcome. I thank Jennifer Crewe and Eric Schwartz at CUP not just for seeking out such careful readers but also for expertly shepherding this project through every stage of its development. I also thank Robert Fellman for his expert copyediting. I remain deeply grateful to the many students from whom I have learned so much in my own sections of Literature Humanities over the years at Columbia.

Finally, and most important: I dedicate this book to the memory of Deborah Martinsen. Deborah initiated the Core Knowledge book series, played a key role in commissioning the first volumes within it, and was in every way a remarkably efficient and hardworking managing editor of the series. It is a source of great sadness that Deborah did not live to see the first fruits of her tireless efforts on behalf of the Core Knowledge initiative. This book is therefore offered as a humble tribute to one who, in the last chapter of her life, endured change with such steadfast courage and belief: Deborah Martinsen.

New York City

June 2022

# On Ovid's *Metamorphoses*

# Introduction

The fall of the Berlin Wall, the rise of the internet, 9/11, the global financial crisis of 2007 and 2008, the murder of George Floyd and the emergence of BLM, COVID-19: momentous events such as these have radically affected so many lives in the last thirty or so years, transforming our daily experience of the world about us and, in the case of the internet in particular, radically affecting how we navigate that world. Our modern experience of change forces us to keep adjusting to circumstance, to expect unforeseen developments, and to face up to the unpredictability that can suddenly destabilize our surest certainties about the world: witness the disruption that COVID-19 suddenly brought to all our lives in March 2020. Where to look for guidance in these uncertain times? We could do a lot worse than turn to Ovid's *Metamorphoses*—or so these pages will try to show in taking you on a brief tour of that remarkable poem of change written just over two thousand years ago. It was composed soon after the Roman Republic had undergone its own great spasm of change that gave rise in the 20s BCE to Rome's new political formation under its first emperor, Augustus. Ovid's *Metamorphoses* was only too sensitive to the breezes of uncertainty that fundamentally conditioned the times in which it was written. This book is about that sensitivity, and about how Ovid's insights into the nature of change itself can still usefully inform and enhance our own twenty-first-century lives.

The fifteen books of the *Metamorphoses*—almost 12,000 lines in all—move from the origins of the world down to Ovid's own times in the decades straddling the first centuries BCE and CE. Along the way, Ovid draws on the vast store of Greco-Roman myth and legend to tell some 250 stories that all have one thing in common: each tale involves change from one physical form into another, such as from human to animal or flower or stone or flowing spring. For some characters, metamorphosis is a reward; for many, a punishment; for others, a means of escape from one mode of existence into another; and for a few, a form of commemoration (so, e.g., Narcissus fades away in death into the flower that today bears his name). But as a general rule, such change is in Ovid's world invariably a one-time event—a permanent state of irreversible transformation. It's also important to bear in mind that a given metamorphosis sometimes appears incidental to the larger thematic or symbolic meaning of an episode, and even an excuse that allows Ovid to build a story around a favored character.

Certainly, metamorphosis gives a form of thematic structure to the poem. But the cascading flow of individual myths across the fifteen books is characterized more by a carefully contrived lack of any rigid structure or by unpredictable shifts of scene, speaker, and storyline across Ovid's narrative. This fluid movement from one story to its often loosely related successor means that it's hard to summarize in any concise way the contents of this endlessly diverse poem. In books 1–10, Ovid ranges widely over the byways of Greco-Roman mythology: after the Creation from chaos and the birth of humankind, the universal flood and the regeneration of mortals later in book 1 move the clock forward from primeval to mythic time and to the erratic, often erotically charged antics of gods and humans. The stories vary considerably in length, and some are coordinated into sequences predicated on place (e.g., Greek Thebes in book 3), theme (e.g., the divine punishment of mortal presumption in book 6), or a single charismatic figure (e.g., the poet Orpheus' song cycle in book 10). Long portions of certain books are dominated by extended treatments of individual gods (e.g., Bacchus in books 3–4), heroes (e.g., Hercules in book 9), and other larger-than-life characters (e.g., Medea in book 7). In books 11–15, Ovid follows a more disciplined chronological path in the quasi-historical portion of the poem: he moves through the Trojan War and the origins of Rome until he finally arrives, late in book 15, in his own times and in the Rome of Augustus.

Ovid was hardly the first Greco-Roman writer to treat the theme of metamorphic myth, but his poem of transformation was itself transformative in the literary landscape of Augustus's Rome. Breathtakingly original in the scale of its intellectual and creative ambition, in many ways it changed the course of Latin literary history through the influence it exerted on successive generations of poets at Rome; and from late antiquity onward, through the Middle Ages and the Renaissance and into the early modern period and far beyond, down to the present day, the work has stood the test of time as one of the most influential cultural legacies of ancient Rome. For present purposes, however, it's important not to lose sight of the sociocultural times in which it was composed in Augustus's Rome. Before proceeding further, then, let's quickly anchor Ovid's *Metamorphoses* in its historical context.

## Ovid, Augustus, and Virgil

Born in 43 BCE in Sulmo (now Sulmona) in central Italy, a provincial town about ninety miles east of Rome, Publius Ovidius Naso belonged to a wealthy and locally prominent family of the so-called equestrian order (i.e., the lower of the two aristocratic classes at Rome, below the senatorial order). He came of age at a critical turning point in Roman history. By the beginning of the 20s BCE, the civil wars that had ravaged the Italian peninsula for much of the last century of the Roman Republic had finally given way to the new institution of the Roman Principate: uncontested power lay with one man, the first emperor Augustus. Born Gaius Octavius in 63 BCE, he became ruler of the republic in 31 BCE and reigned as Augustus, his acquired name, from 27 BCE to his death in 14 CE. When his great-uncle, the dictator Julius Caesar, was assassinated on the Ides of March 44 BCE, the young Octavius was designated in Caesar's will as his adopted son and heir, and he became Gaius Julius Caesar Octavianus (he's also commonly known as Octavian in English). After further convulsions in the 30s BCE, Marcus Antonius (as in Shakespeare's *Antony and Cleopatra*), Octavian's great rival, was decisively defeated at the Battle of Actium in 31 BCE. With that victory Octavian in effect brought the long-term Roman Clash of the Titans to a close.

But how to begin healing a hopelessly fractured state? Octavian was careful to present himself as no autocrat but as the first citizen, or *princeps*—hence the term Principate—of what was presented as his revival of embedded republican institutions. In January 27 BCE, the Roman senate conferred on him the title Augustus, a name with strong religious and moral connotations and an etymological connection to the Latin verb *augere* ("to increase")—a suitable title for one whose mission it was to revive and rebuild Rome after the trauma of the previous decades. The age of Augustus ushered in a period of relative calm and stability in which the emperor himself remained ostensibly committed to republican procedures and institutions even as he ruled as a de facto dictator. Further civic and religious honors and offices consolidated his authority at the heart of the state, and the development of a full-blown Augustan ideology at Rome was based on that central foundation.

It was in the first years of Augustus's rise to undisputed power that Ovid came of age and began his prolific career as one of ancient Rome's most distinguished poets. As a young man of precocious talent Ovid quickly found fame as a love poet in the Roman tradition of erotic elegy, and he constantly tested the conventions of the genre through restless experimentation with inherited forms. His *Art of Love* was especially provocative: written in three books probably between 2 BCE and 2 CE, this parody of a poem of instruction taught both men (books 1 and 2) and women (book 3) how to find and keep a lover. It drew Augustus's eye but also his ire. Early in his reign his program of renewal at Rome soon extended to the moral sphere. Beyond the high infant mortality rate, decades of civil war had significantly depleted the male population, and it had to be regenerated. But Augustus also saw great symbolic capital in the restoration of traditional Roman values and morality. Hence he introduced legislation to promote marriage and procreation and to discourage adultery, and it was in the context of this moral reform that the *Art of Love* courted controversy. In 8 CE, the emperor banished Ovid from Rome to Tomis, modern Constanta, on the western coast of the Black Sea in what is now Romania; Ovid was never to return to the metropolis and died in exile, probably in 17 CE. But why punish Ovid for his risqué poem of love only six or so years after it came into circulation? There were in fact two causes of his banishment: beyond the alleged immorality of his *Art of Love*, the second, apparently more immediate cause was a mysterious blunder by which Ovid personally offended Augustus. Ovid often alludes to this fateful mistake in his poetic writings in exile, but he never discloses its full nature.

Written in the years before his banishment in 8 CE, the *Metamorphoses* was by far Ovid's largest-scale undertaking and his only major composition in the so-called dactylic hexameter—the meter of those archetypal Greek epics, the *Iliad* and the *Odyssey*, and synonymous with the Greco-Roman poetic tradition of martial epic from Homer onward. Ovid may have partially revised the *Metamorphoses* after he was exiled, but the poem was substantially complete before his banishment. Life and art converged all too tragically in his downfall: the poet of transformation was himself transformed by the trauma of his exile.

Against this background, Augustus casts an omnipresent shadow over the four chapters that follow. He was as much a symbol as a living ruler at Rome: he was an all-penetrating presence and phenomenon who left his mark on every aspect of Roman social, cultural, religious, and political life. His image and imprint were everywhere, on coins, on public statues and monuments, in architecture, in the Roman festival calendar, in religious practices and legislative edicts. Augustus was also charismatic and enigmatic as both a novelty and a contradiction. As the upholder of republican tradition but a de facto autocrat, he hovered ambiguously between republican and imperial images of authority. Nonmonarchical and nondictatorial by appearance, he was in reality Rome's undisputed strongman and power conductor.

Like Augustus, the *Metamorphoses* is in its own way a unique phenomenon that's hard to categorize by any ordinary terms of generic definition. It's an epic in its length, in its meter, and in its breadth of ambition in moving all the way from the creation of the world at the start of book 1 down to the age of Augustus at the end of book 15. Yet it's hardly a conventional epic in its frequent lightness of touch and tone, in its subject matter (there's really very little in the way of traditional epic warring in the poem), and in its nonlinear and often meandering style of storytelling. But if Augustus symbolized Rome's reconsolidation after decades of civil strife and if the Age of Augustus was all about building a new political stability, the worldview projected by the *Metamorphoses* in many ways runs counter to that process of stabilization. Certainly, Ovid praises Augustus to the skies in his poem of change, and when Augustus is destined for the skies in his promised deification at the end of book 15, that transformation into a god is the crowning metamorphosis of the entire poem. Augustus's adoptive father, Julius Caesar, had been the first historical Roman to be officially deified when, in 42 BCE, he was posthumously granted the title "Divine Julius" by the Roman senate. Augustus was similarly declared a god after his death in 14 CE, but already in life he allowed himself to be recognized as a living god—hence Ovid's knowing portrayals of Augustus's immanent and imminent divinity in the *Metamorphoses*. But it's hard not to detect certain signs of ironic skepticism in these flattering touches—a questioning tendency that's typical of the deeper meaning of the *Metamorphoses* beneath the attractions of its surface storytelling.

Ovid's accent on changefulness, unpredictability, the potential deceptiveness of appearances, and the fickle ways of the gods is sharply provocative in the context of this Roman resurgence under Augustus. It's as if Ovid, that self-appointed emperor in his own world of words, asserts a vision of mutability that directly challenges the steadying influence of the official commander in chief, Augustus. But another striking feature of the poem is that so many of the characters who populate its episodes are outsiders, misfits, eccentrics, troublemakers, obsessives, and persecuted artists. What caused Ovid to go in this direction? We've already observed that he died in exile. But in a sense he was always an exile—an outsider in Augustus's Rome, and increasingly so as time went on and the regime became more paranoid about message control and less tolerant of free expression, at least in egregious cases (it's surely an overstatement to say that Augustus clamped down on free speech in any systematic and exhaustive way). His pen was distinctive, provocative, nonconformist, and idiosyncratic: *this* is the Ovid who takes center stage in the four chapters that follow.

Apart from Augustus, however, another figure casts a long shadow over these pages: Virgil (70–19 BCE), the celebrated author of, among other great works, the epic *Aeneid* in twelve books. Virgil composed this poem in the last decade or so of his life and left it partially unfinished at his death. Rooted in the Greco-Roman epic tradition extending all the way back to Homer, the *Aeneid* was recognized in Virgil's own lifetime as a landmark in the history of Latin poetics—a monumental production that vied on the Roman side with the cultural stature of the *Iliad* and the *Odyssey* on the Greek side.

The *Aeneid* tells the story of the hero Aeneas's departure from his native Troy after it was destroyed by the Greeks at the end of the Trojan War. Aeneas's divinely sanctioned destiny is to reach Italy, where his descendants are fated to found the new Troy in the shape of Rome. Augustus is presented in the *Aeneid* as Aeneas's distant but destined successor as Rome's champion in a new golden age of peace and prosperity. Despite its purple passages of adulation, however, few readers would now find in the *Aeneid* a straightforward endorsement of Rome's greatness under Augustus. The *Aeneid* is far too nuanced in its sociopolitical sensitivities to offer anything like an uncritical or hopelessly idealized portrayal of Aeneas as a forerunner of Augustus, as Ovid would have been the first to recognize. But Virgil's vision of Rome's fated rise from the ashes of Troy nevertheless coincides with the narrative of reconsolidation and renewal that Augustus's regime never ceased to project. For this reason, the *Aeneid* offers an important touchstone for "Romanness" as constructed and propagated under Augustus, and even as realized in his carefully cultivated public image.

Beyond Augustus, then, Virgil's *Aeneid* looms large in this book as a major catalyst for reaction and response in the *Metamorphoses*. Indeed, in many ways Ovid's poem of change can be productively viewed as a respectful but provocative counter-text to the *Aeneid*. Take the temporal span of the *Aeneid* from Troy's fall to the foretold golden age of Augustus's Rome: Ovid progresses toward a similar endpoint in Augustus in *Metamorphoses* 15, but he dwarfs the *Aeneid* in the process. This is how the *Metamorphoses* begins:

> Changes of shape, new forms, are the theme which my
>     spirit impels me
> now to recite. Inspire me, O gods (it is you who have even
> transformed my art), and spin me a thread from the world's
>     beginning
> *down to my own lifetime*, in one continuous poem.
>
>                                                          (1.1–4)

The twelve-book *Aeneid* takes its starting point from 1184 BCE (by one influential ancient estimate, the year of Troy's fall). But in beginning from the Creation in *Metamorphoses* 1, Ovid first forms the world that Augustus will ultimately master when the poet gets "down to my own lifetime" in book 15. Ovid's fifteen books thus amount to a supersized expansion of Virgil's dozen, but the further implication is that the *Aeneid* is relatively parochial in scale and scope in comparison with Ovid's own bigger-picture poetics. This pushy expansion of horizons suggests that for Ovid nothing—not even Virgil's hallowed achievement in the *Aeneid*—is sacred or beyond challenge.

The view of the *Metamorphoses* offered in these pages is inseparable from the larger sociocultural climate and literary context that Augustus and Virgil did so much to mold and influence in Ovid's day. But this focus on conditions at Rome when Ovid composed his poem of change is only half of the story that's told in our four chapters. The other half centers on the *Metamorphoses* as a text of our times—a living and breathing meditation on the human condition that's of direct relevance to so many aspects of modern-day experience.

## Reading Ovid with 2020s Vision

What work can the *Metamorphoses* do with and for us now, in the twenty-first century? How might it open our eyes and inform our lives amid the changeful uncertainties of the fast-paced, globally connected world that surrounds us? Nowadays, the *Metamorphoses* is well enough known in the popular imagination as a storehouse of Greco-Roman mythology, and it's often read for the entertainment value of its individual stories. But what to look for and how to find it when we delve into the text a little more deeply?

Two broad tendencies in the *Metamorphoses* will figure prominently in what follows. On the one hand, there's self-discovery and experimentation: Ovid features a vast array of different human identities, natures, and orientations (sexual, behavioral, temperamental, ideological, etc.) in a narrative of endless diversity, unfettered speech, and freedom of thought and action. On the other hand, many stories tell of speech that's shut down, artists persecuted, minds frozen into intransigence: Ovid's world of change feels so much harsher and colder when this negative strain of behavior takes hold. All the while, Ovid's characters often talk, declaim, bluster, converse, and hold court in different styles and layers of speech that continually test the nature of truth telling. Sound bite, extended discourse, formal declaration, unverifiable assertion, more or less transparent fakery:

these and other speech acts in the poem need careful parsing so that truth can be told from falsehood, ulterior motives may be sniffed out, and we can decipher what a given character is really saying and for what reason. Among so much more, the *Metamorphoses* offers an education in how to guard against the slippery enticements of the modern news media, the seductive superficialities of social media, and the chicanery of so much online fiction peddling.

In the last century, Ovid has often been perceived as a lesser poet in comparison with Virgil in particular: more Mozart than Beethoven, so to speak. True, the playfulness of Ovid's verbal manner can give the impression that he prizes rhetorical effects for their own sake, that he values style over substance, and that he goes out of his way to reject accepted truths and certainties in favor of a mannered irony and a relativist skepticism about the world. These features of his writing are in many ways undeniable. But it's also important not to underestimate the profundity that often underlies—and can even be deliberately camouflaged by—these surface tendencies. In the last four or so decades, a forward-looking generation of readers has increasingly found in Ovid an ancient author who touches on certain sociocultural tendencies that find suggestive points of comparison in our own time. He inevitably reflects many unappealing features of Roman life, the most obvious among them being institutional slavery and a deep-seated culture of violence, especially against women. But he's also been lauded as protofeminist in certain ways, nonjudgmental about sexual orientation, and laser-like in exposing the hypocrisy of ruling elites. He's been viewed as healthily ironic and questioning rather than literal minded and lamely wedded (or resigned) to the status quo. His is a floating intelligence rather than one that's dogmatic and univocal—in terms of Augustus's Rome, a breath of fresh air, with an independence of vision and an outspokenness that have struck a chord with his modern readership.

Four mutually informing approaches to the poem are offered in our four chapters. First, Ovid's eye for individuality: chapter 1 focuses on the ever-shifting diversity of characterization in the *Metamorphoses* as different figures undergo their own highly idiosyncratic forms of psychological, sexual, or emotional awakening or evolution. If Augustus promoted a certain typology of "Romanness," Ovid moves in a different direction by exploring many varied and often empowering assertions of selfhood in his ever-changeful cast of characters. Second, the mutability of speech and language in Ovid's world of words in the *Metamorphoses*: in chapter 2 we'll sample how changefulness is embedded in the very fabric of his text, especially through tonal ambiguity and subtle, often ironic shadings of meaning. Ovid carefully cultivates this slipperiness of words, and in many ways this chapter will be concerned with the object lesson that he offers in how to negotiate an environment—Augustus's Rome as much as ours—in which the "truth" is so often a verbal construction and an instrument of power and all too often not to be taken at face value. This attention to linguistic control will also help us appreciate what's lost, or at least hard to convey, when Ovid's Latin is read in translation.

Third, Ovid's portrayal of unsettling behavioral extremes in the *Metamorphoses*: as one major illustration of this phenomenon, chapter 3 focuses on two notorious tales of incest that he recounts at length in the heart of the poem. These stories partly showcase Ovid's penchant for provocatively exploring unconventional, disturbing, or deviant mindsets in the *Metamorphoses*. But they also demonstrate how changes of perspective on the reader's part—seeing a given story from a different or unusual angle—can transform our understanding of that episode. Finally, in chapter 4, we turn to the shifting and inconsistent picture of how justice is dispensed in the rough-and-tumble world of the *Metamorphoses*, especially justice as administered by the gods. As we saw earlier, Augustus was recognized as a god in his own lifetime and officially deified after his death. When we witness the erratic workings of divine justice in the *Metamorphoses*, it's hard to avoid reflecting on how justice operates at Rome under the godlike Augustus, and harder still to forget Ovid's own experience of Augustan retribution in 8 CE. Hence our task in chapter 4 is to explore Ovid's banishment—his personal catastrophe and metamorphosis—in relation to his treatment of crime and punishment in the *Metamorphoses*.

This little book ends in chapter 4, then, with Augustus's crushing of the butterfly that was Ovid—nimble of movement, ever flitting in his flutter-by suggestiveness, delighting the senses and appealing to the imagination but always elusive and hard to capture in words. The first three chapters show the butterfly in flight until, in the last chapter, Ovid falls to earth. Our overall story is partly about that downfall and partly about how and why the *Metamorphoses* can help us find our way through our changeful twenty-first-century times.

# 1

# Diversity, Idiosyncrasy, and Self-Discovery in the *Metamorphoses*

How to do justice to the sheer range and diversity of the larger-than-life characters who populate the *Metamorphoses*—their quirks of behavior, sexual proclivities, eccentric tendencies, conditionings of temperament, and so on? The claim of this chapter isn't just that Ovid's eye for idiosyncratic character formation reflects his endless powers of invention and psychological exploration. We've already touched on some of the ways in which Augustus promoted a particular vision of "Romanness" as part of his reconstruction effort after decades of civil strife. Virgil's Aeneas has his limitations and flaws, but in many respects he is a model of such "Romanness." To illustrate the point, a virtue much paraded by Augustus was *pietas*, or dutiful loyalty to the gods, country, and family, especially parents; it's no accident that the adjective *pius* is synonymous with Virgil's Aeneas or that his devotion to his father, Anchises, is a central preoccupation of the *Aeneid*. But if we associate a certain forging of character and values with Rome's renewal under Augustus, the explosion of characterful diversity that we find in the *Metamorphoses* reveals a different tendency—a process not so much of typological formation but of released individuality.

This chapter is centrally concerned with the *Metamorphoses* as a counter-reaction of sorts to the forces of what might loosely be called this Roman ideological shaping of character under Augustus. Virgil helps us get the show on the road before we turn to a series of case studies that will illustrate Ovid's preoccupation with nonconformity, self-discovery, and the strong expression of individuality, often at a remove from societally accepted or ordained codes of behavior. For its times, and despite its rootedness in a slave society that was conservative, male dominated, and generally rigid in its patriarchal structures, the *Metamorphoses* is in many ways a remarkably flexible, liberating, and open-minded text. Loosely to invoke modern terminology, it's a suggestively progressive work.

## Aeneas in Virgil, Ovid on Aeneas

Ovid's Aeneas has a tough act to follow: how different, how metamorphosed, is he from his superstar counterpart in Virgil? For help with this question, let's consult the priestess known as the Cumaean Sibyl—by legend, the priestess who presided over the temple of Apollo at Cumae, a Greek colony near Naples in Italy. In the *Aeneid*, the Sibyl guides Aeneas on his descent to the Underworld to visit his now-deceased father. She recurs late in the *Metamorphoses*, in Ovid's mischievously brief treatment (barely five lines on the trip down and back up!) of that hallowed Virgilian episode.

This is how Ovid's Sibyl replies to Aeneas's prayer for guidance to the Underworld in *Metamorphoses* 14:

"You ask great things, you greatest of heroes, whose valour

was proved by your sword in the fray and whose love as a
    son and a father

was tested by fire. But, noble Trojan, you need not be
    troubled.

Your prayer shall be granted and I shall guide you to
    Pluto's realm,

where you'll see the Elysian Fields and meet your father's
    dear spirit.

No path is closed to the virtuous man."

(14.108–13)

The Latin for "you greatest of heroes" in line 108 is *vir factis maxime*, literally "man greatest in deeds"; but when we look for those deeds, those *facta*, earlier in the *Metamorphoses*, they're not so easy to find. When we first encounter Aeneas in Book 13, we find him making his exit from the inferno of Troy, his father, Anchises, on his shoulders and his son Ascanius at his side. Ovid duly calls Aeneas *pius* ("dutiful" [13.626]), thereby anointing him with his defining characteristic in Virgil. But then it's all travelogue as Aeneas takes to the seas and our hero makes what largely amounts to a whistle-stop tour of the various places that he visited en route for Italy in the early books of the *Aeneid*. Along the way, Ovid spices things up by inserting various diverting stories of transformation—a welcome relief from the checklist feel as Aeneas just keeps going from location to location. Who can forget Aeneas's love affair with the beautiful Carthaginian queen Dido in *Aeneid* 4 and her tragic suicide after Aeneas suddenly abandons her to pursue his divinely ordained mission to found the new Troy in Italy? Well, Ovid's Aeneas hardly seems to dwell painfully on the tragedy that he leaves in his wake: the storyline of *Aeneid* 4 is compressed into four lines of quick-fire summation as Dido "built a funeral pyre on false religious pretences, / and fell on her sword, so cheating the world as she had been cheated" (14.80–81). In Ovid's telling, this is hardly an affair that reflects well on Aeneas as part-time lover, that "man greatest in deeds."

At last Aeneas reaches Italy and consults the Sibyl at Cumae. She proceeds to guide him to the Underworld, and, as book 14 progresses, Ovid continues to lead us through the Virgilian storyline until he squeezes the essence of *Aeneid* 7 through 12 into a five-line miracle of compression (14.449–53). In this passage, Turnus, the formidable native Italian warrior prince, fights it out with the newcomer Aeneas. Aeneas duly triumphs in that heavyweight matchup, but in contrast to Virgil's climactic account of the same duel in the last book of the *Aeneid*, Ovid makes little of Aeneas's victory ("Turnus fell in the battle" [573]). He also tactfully (or shamelessly?) passes in silence over Aeneas's troubling murder of his rival when, in Virgil, the vanquished Turnus lies prostrate and helpless before him; more on that in a moment. And when Aeneas is subsequently made a god, it's largely because his mother, Venus, petitions Jupiter effectively on his behalf, not least by arguing that "he already has seen the unlovely / kingdom of Hades and crossed the Styx. Is once not enough?" (590–91). So much for any track record of valiant *facta* that speaks compellingly for itself, simply requiring to be rewarded with apotheosis.

The key point in all this? Ovid's Aeneas is a decaffeinated version of Virgil's original, a pale shadow who struggles to live up to the "noble Trojan" hailed by the Sibyl in *Metamorphoses* 14. Already in the *Aeneid* Aeneas strays from his destiny to found the new Troy in Italy when he engages in his dalliance with Dido in Carthage. But when Mercury visits him there in *Aeneid* 4, delivering a reminder from Jupiter of Aeneas's duty to his fated mission to Italy, a change comes: from that point on, Aeneas takes on a more blinkered obedience to his responsibility, as if the claims of self and free will have given way once and for all to the call of destiny. True, Aeneas still shows flashes of spontaneous passion. Anchises had solemnly impressed upon his son the Roman way in *Aeneid* 6:

> ". . . but yours will be the rulership of nations,
> remember, Roman, these will be your arts:
> to teach the ways of peace to those you conquer,
> to spare defeated peoples, tame the proud."
>
> (6.851–53; trans. A. Mandelbaum)

But Aeneas forgets that precept when, at the very end of the *Aeneid*, the red mists of fury descend and, far from sparing the defeated Turnus, he cold-bloodedly murders him to avenge the death at Turnus's hands of Pallas, Aeneas's young protégé. This explosion of impassioned violence vastly complicates the *Aeneid* by undoing, in the poem's last lines, the grip of self-discipline and commitment to duty that the epic has gradually enforced in its leading player: the disturbing ending reaffirms Aeneas's taciturnity even as (or because) it shatters the demeanor we've become so used to in him for such a long stretch of the *Aeneid*.

What Ovid gives us is an exaggerated version of the disciplined and subdued, on-message Aeneas who prevails for most of the *Aeneid* after book 4. As in Virgil, Ovid's Aeneas carries Anchises from the burnt-out Troy, but Aeneas then becomes very much the carried in Ovid's seaborne narrative—a gentle parody, perhaps, of what Ovid saw as Aeneas's passivity for much of the *Aeneid*. Let's now take up the point that Virgil had already configured Aeneas as, in many ways, an embodiment of "the good Roman" in the age of Augustus. Even when Aeneas strays at the end of the *Aeneid* from the qualities of mercy and controlled aggression as inculcated in him by Anchises in the Underworld, that aberration can still illustrate a positive ethos through a negative departure from it. But if the *Aeneid* is centripetal in this respect, drawing us to a core vision of what it means to be Roman, the *Metamorphoses* is far more centrifugal in its tendency to release and empower different and often quirky or misfit facets of personality. One of the most conspicuous, and attractive, features of the poem is how multiple characters embrace and assert their own natures regardless of outside (and sometimes internal) forces that try to repress, repel, or control those natures.

In prizing the individual essence over conformity to type in such cases, the *Metamorphoses* may well strike twenty-first-century readers as very relatable, at least in certain but significant ways, to the modern moment in liberal democracies like the United States. Diversity initiatives are gradually bringing a new equality of opportunity and representation in the workplace and in public life. Serious efforts are at last being made to address the prejudices that historically favored the few by disfavoring people of color, the LGBTQ+ community, and adherents of "other" religions or cultural affiliations. Of course, all talk of Ovid's accent on personal liberation and self-expression has to be set against the sobering reality that he was writing in a slave society, and it would be glib to overstate the lines of connectivity between then and now, Ovid's time and ours, when the *Metamorphoses* is evidently rooted in a culture that's so distant from our own. It's important to tread carefully, then; but in a modern context where the new empowerment of hitherto marginalized groups is beginning to challenge the old order on multiple fronts, Ovid's interest in self-realization at the individual level strikes a timely chord. True also, the voices of the "other" often struggle to contend against entrenched forces of repression and vindictiveness, as we'll see when we sample in chapter 4 how cruelly Ovid's gods all too often treat mortals in the *Metamorphoses*. In this respect, it would be misleading to cast the poem as anything like a straightforward anthem to self-discovery and effortless self-liberation. But the green shoots of a keenly felt individuality nevertheless remain conspicuously visible in multiple episodes across the fifteen books—in many cases, a restless individuality that is just waiting to erupt.

And so to the three test cases of individual self-discovery that we'll explore in this chapter: first, the self-absorbed Narcissus in book 3; then Medea's growth to maturity in book 7, as she evolves from her girlhood in Colchis (now western Georgia in the Black Sea region) to become a cosmopolitan murderess who wreaks havoc in Greece; and we turn finally to one of the most intimate areas in which individuality asserts itself in the *Metamorphoses*: gender and sexuality, with our focus for now mainly on gender change (Ovid's interest in diverse aspects of sexuality will be taken up in chapter 3). But first things first: let's reflect on Narcissus's self-reflection in book 3.

## The Eyes Have It: Narcissus's Self-Regard

Catastrophic mistakes abound in *Metamorphoses* 3 even before we get to Narcissus's self-delusion. Poor Actaeon, so unlucky in his fateful error when, early in the book, he stumbles upon Diana, the goddess of hunting, as she bathes with her nymphs in a woodland spring! He sees her naked, she sees red, and he incurs her naked anger: she transforms him into a voiceless stag, and he is soon hounded to death by his own hunting dogs. The mistakes proliferate when we read on and find Semele duped by Juno into asking Jupiter to reveal himself to his new lover "in all the majestic splendour he shows / when he comes to the arms of Juno, dressed in his full regalia" (285–86); Semele is burned to a crisp when Jupiter flashes his bolt and blasts her boudoir with "his everyday missile" (305). Then the hallowed Greek seer Teiresias: who enjoys sex more, the male or the female partner? Juno and Jupiter debate the question and finally consult Teiresias for expert advice—he's known both sides after spending seven years as a woman. It's the woman, says Teiresias, adjudicating in Jupiter's favor; Juno resents the verdict and condemns Teiresias to blindness, thereby opening his eyes to the fickle spitefulness of divine retribution. All this in the way of missteps and accidental misjudgments in the tragicomedy of error in book 3 before we encounter one who's a rather more blameworthy architect of his own misfortune: Narcissus.

The storyline: a young nymph, Echo, helps her fellow nymphs by holding Juno in conversation just when the goddess is on the warpath, trying to catch Jupiter in yet more of his illicit trysts. Echo buys the nymphs time to get away undetected, but she pays for it when Juno punishes her prattling: "Echo could only repeat the words she heard at the end / of a sentence and never reply for herself" (368–69). She falls in love with Narcissus, that beautiful boy, but he harshly rejects her. Still pining for him, she wastes away until she becomes voice alone, echo instead of Echo. Narcissus arrogantly rejects his female and male admirers alike until one of them prays for payback: may Narcissus fall in love and never gain the object of his desire! He falls for his own reflection when he sees himself in a mirrorlike pool—after Actaeon's encounter with Diana, another disastrous error of seeing, but this time a delusion that punishes Narcissus's arrogance. He echoes Echo in pining away at his own reflection and in wasting away to virtually nothing, as if becoming as insubstantial as the image that keeps him riveted. But then a flash of recognition: "I know you now and I know myself," Narcissus exclaims (463), as if a sudden convert to the Socratic call of "Know thyself!" But he has no route of escape from his self-obsession apart from fading away to become the flower that bears his name, his enduring reflection in death.

This story is hardly the first in the *Metamorphoses* to explore the nature (or absence) of self-knowledge. In book 2, for but one example, Apollo's son, Phaethon, asks for confirmation of his paternity, and Daddy responds by overcompensating as an anxious-to-please überparent: "Now ask me whatever favour you will, / and I shall bestow it" (44–45). Phaethon asks to drive his father's sun chariot for a day, and the god can't retract his promise; Phaethon doesn't know what he's getting into, Apollo has badly misread the situation, and disaster inevitably follows when the feckless youth crashes the chariot and a vast conflagration seizes the earth. But the Narcissus episode is the first in which Ovid explicitly features the psychology of self-delusion in a dedicated, front-and-center fashion. The episode thrives on paradox and irony, with a yawning gulf between Narcissus's lack of self-knowledge and the artistic self-consciousness with which Ovid exposes the shallowness of his own creation.

The patterns of paradox and deceptive reflection run deep as Narcissus looks into the pool and is scorched by what he sees ("the sight . . . fires him with passion" [3.430]), as if water for once has the ability to ignite. While he sees his own image, he also partly reflects Echo in being a prisoner to vision as she is to voice; and yet there's no echo when, he complains, he can watch the exquisite lips of his own reflection "gently repeating / my words—but I never can *hear* you repeat them!" (461–62). Through this lip movement his words are there to be inferred by seeing, not listening, in a displacement of sight and sound—a blurring of categories that's also felt in the confusion of image and reality when Narcissus at first fails to register the emptiness of his own reflection. This failure to heed himself is reflected in the ironies that Ovid brilliantly builds into Narcissus's choice of words. "I've looked and have longed," cries Narcissus. "But looking and longing is far from enough. / I still have to find! [*quod videoque placetque / non tamen invenio*]" (446–47). The finding will be impossible, we know, but he can't see the illusory reality even as it stares him in the face. This division of self is brought out with a poignant beauty in Ovid's Latin: the word *quod* (the relative pronoun "which/what") stands in ambiguous relation to the two verbs that it simultaneously accompanies, as a nominative subject in the one case (*quod . . . placet*, "what pleases") and as an accusative object in the other (*quod . . . video*, "what I see"). Narcissus himself is here configured as a grammatical schizophrenic, a subject/object viewer who's viewed.

This fusion of identities is also expressed more than once through his use of the royal "We" in first-person-plural verb forms. Take lines 451–52:

> Whenever I move to kiss
> the clear bright surface, his upturned face strains closer
> to mine.

Here is a fine example of what is lost when Ovid's Latin is read in translation. "I move to kiss" corresponds to *porreximus oscula* in the original, but the Latin first-person-plural verb is rendered in the English singular. From one angle, Narcissus uses the royal "We" conventionally enough here. But what he doesn't recognize is that his plural verb captures the plurality of his self and image all too accurately as both he and his reflection move in for a kiss that is frustratingly unilateral on both sides: the act is shared, but it's just lip service, as neither kiss truly lands.

At last Narcissus realizes that he's his own reflection, and from this moment on he takes self-conscious ownership of the ironies that have hitherto crept inadvertently into his words. "What can I do? Must I woo or be wooed? What else can I plead for? / All I desire I have" (465–66): in "woo or be wooed," the passive and active forms of the same Latin verb (*roger anne rogem?*) neatly bring out the dialogical interplay between subject and object, albeit with a new confusion as to which takes precedence. Is Narcissus's reflection now the dominant subject, as if he's metamorphosed into his own mirror image (an implication beautifully captured by Kevin Richard in figure 1) before his ultimate transformation into a flower? But he's at his most philosophical when he has this to say:

**Figure 1.** Kevin P. Richard, *Echoes of a Perennial Narcissus*, 2014.
*Source*: Copyright Kevin Richard. www.oldsoulart.com

Oh, how I wish that I and my body could now be parted,
I wish my love were not here!—a curious prayer for a lover.
Now my sorrow is sapping my strength. My life is almost
over. Its candle is guttering out in the prime of my manhood.
Death will be easy to bear, since dying will cure my
   heartache.

(3.467–71)

We've already witnessed the Socrates in Narcissus, in the "Know
thyself!" moment when he recognizes himself in his reflection.
But the tragedy of his death wish here is mixed with a tinge of
philosophical yearning, as if he recalls in line 467 Socrates's
portrayal in Plato's *Phaedo* of death releasing the immortal soul

from its bodily incarceration in life. Then there's the strange detachment of self that enables him to craft, just as the first waves of his identity crisis begin to crash upon him, the polished one-liner in 468. In the Latin, *vellem quod amamus abesset*, the royal "We" in *amamus* repeats the trick of conflating Narcissus's ego and alter ego, but this time he seemingly does it knowingly, and, paradoxically, the separation from self that he wishes for in *abesset* amounts to a craving for union—a severance that joins.

This is a cul-de-sac of a story: it features a revelatory moment of self-discovery, yes, but it offers no scope for personal growth or transformation on the basis of that discovery. The pool in which Narcissus fatally saw his reflection is idyllic to behold but chilling in its lifeless sterility, in a landscape unvisited by any bird or beast—a perfect setting for the death knell of a storyline that's devoid of all flesh-and-blood vitality or any progressive deepening of self-knowledge beyond Narcissus's realization that he's his own reflection. This lack of individual development is a widespread phenomenon in the *Metamorphoses*: the sad tales of Phaethon or Semele, say, end in their destruction, not in any gradual growth toward maturity; Actaeon's death is spitefully vindictive, and he's granted no shot at redemption for his mistake before he's turned into a stag and torn apart by his own hounds. It's a matter of time: when Ovid builds a greater temporal span into his storylines, his characters have more scope for maturation before our eyes, they take on more layers of personality, and Ovid's portraiture delves deeper. His extended treatment of Medea in the first half of book 7 marks something of a turning point in the poem in this respect. After dwelling on Narcissus's surface reflection, let's now follow

Medea's life story as she gradually evolves from teen to killing machine in this lengthy episode—perhaps the closest Ovid comes in the *Metamorphoses* to a Rembrandt of a pen portrait.

## The Making of a Murderess: Medea and Moreness

Ovid's Medea in book 7 is a law unto herself, a ruthless killer who's capable even of murdering her own children. But even though her appetite for blood is chilling, she can arguably claim mitigating circumstances and provocations for at least some (even many?) of her actions. As she takes to the skies and soars from place to place and from one exploit to the next, she in any case symbolically flies above the law at ground level. And all along she never ceases to fascinate because she always poses the question: what on earth might she do next?

Let's start at the end of the episode and work backward—a fitting approach given Medea's skill in causing rivers to run backward (199–200). Medea is almost literally a central figure in the *Metamorphoses*: her story is located more or less bang in the middle of the poem; and she goes out with a bang when, as her final exploit in book 7, she tries to murder the Greek hero Theseus, the son of Aegeus, king of Athens. Medea has fairly recently arrived in Athens, and she's now Aegeus's wife. The attempt on Theseus's life is truly shocking for at least two reasons. First, though Theseus is Aegeus's son, Aegeus doesn't know it. Medea is set on killing him for a reason or reasons that Ovid doesn't explain. One unstated possibility is that she senses a threat to the fortunes of Medus, her own son with Aegeus; hence Theseus has to be disposed of, and she persuades Aegeus that the young man is his enemy. But it bears repeating that Ovid gives no hint of this motive in his treatment of the episode, saying only that she's "bent on his murder" (406): could it be that she needs no motive other than the thrill of the kill? Second, Medea's murder weapon of choice is in a sense Aegeus himself; is the further thrill that she manages to murder remotely? She induces Aegeus to hand Theseus a poisoned chalice. Theseus is about to drink from it when Aegeus spots his own family emblem engraved on the hilt of the young man's sword. Realizing that he is Theseus's father, he dashes the cup from his son's lips; joyful that Theseus is safe, he's nevertheless "filled with horror that such a terrible crime / had been so closely prevented" (426–27). Medea's cunning plan is foiled, but she's nowhere to be seen. She's gone in a flash not just from Aegeus's palace but also from Ovid's *Metamorphoses*, where there's no further trace of her. What's her next destination going to be, we wonder, and what's her next trick as, we imagine, her magical mystery tour continues?

Medea inevitably carries a great weight of literary baggage when she makes her entry in book 7, most obviously because of her notoriety as the killer of her own children. According to the story best known from the fifth-century BCE Greek *Medea* of Euripides, Jason had traveled on the first ship ever built, the Argo, to her native Colchis to filch the Golden Fleece; he's accompanied by his swarthy band of heroes, the so-called Argonauts. Medea soon falls in love with Jason. After using her magic to help him snatch the Fleece, she accompanies him back to Greece as his bride, only for him to abandon her for a Greek princess. Medea takes vengeance by sending, via her own children, a poisoned robe that kills the princess, and she completes her revenge against Jason by subsequently killing those children.

Ovid had already treated the myth twice before, in his own Latin *Medea* tragedy, which is now lost, and in one of his so-called *Heroides* poems, or elegiac letters purporting to be sent from famous heroines (*heroides* in Latin) to their lovers—Penelope to Odysseus, for example, or Dido to Aeneas. We're to imagine that Medea's letter to Jason, the twelfth in the *Heroides* collection, is penned after he's decided to abandon her for the Greek princess. We can't know what kind of character development Medea underwent in Ovid's lost *Medea*, but the *Heroides* letter ends on an ominous note when she has this to say in her closing line: "Certainly, something greater [*maius*] is stirring in my mind!" This "something greater" is her terrible act of infanticide: it's as if she writes her elegiac letter in anticipation of the tragedy that will unfold in Ovid's *Medea*. But her allusion to "something greater" also anticipates a central character trait that she shows in *Metamorphoses* 7: a restless appetite always for *moreness*—ever more experimentation with her magic, ever more nuance to her cunning machinations, ever further extremes of outrageous accomplishment. Can we see shades of Ovid's own ceaseless literary imagination in this endlessly inventive Medea? If so, Medea may prove to be an Ovidian Muse of sorts—at least, that is, until an extraordinary rift seems to emerge between the poet and his leading lady.

When we first encounter Medea in book 7, she's falling in love with Jason but just about manages to hold her desire in check. Yet from the outset she shows a certain ambition for moreness in sensing the advantages of helping Jason and his fellow Greeks to get the Fleece: they are her ticket out of

the "barbarous land" of Colchis (53) to the civilized trappings
of Greece, so that in leaving her homeland she'll "not forsake
greatness / but rather pursue it" (55–56). We find her next in a
shadowy grove, at "the ancient altar of Hecate, / goddess of spells"
(74–75), where Jason just happens (really?) to appear on the scene:
he applies his tough-guy charm, she's infatuated, and with the
help of her magic he manages to capture the Fleece. They return
to Greece, now married, but he seems prouder of the Fleece than
he is of Medea, who more resembles cargo on the Argo. She's
saved his life, but he wastes no time in asking for her help once
more: can she use her magic to take a few years off his own life
and transfer them to his elderly father, Aeson? He again appeals
to her sense of ambition: she'll not just meet his request but sur-
pass it by doing him the "even greater favor" (*maius munus* in the
Latin: always more!) by rejuvenating Aeson with no loss to Jason's
own years.

For nine days and nights Medea goes on tour through the
mountains and byways of Greece, collecting the exotic herbs
that she needs for her formidable new challenge. In contrast to
the parochial girl in Colchis who was fearful of taking to the
seas, she now takes to the skies with a mature confidence, as if
now truly a witch of the world. When she boils up her rejuvenating brew, her appetite for moreness again reveals itself in her
meticulous attention to detail and her adding, adding, adding
of every conceivable refinement to her concoction:

> With these and a thousand nameless objects, the Colchian
>     witch
> was ready to work her spell transcending the powers of a
>     mortal.

> Dipping the branch of an olive, once fruitful but long since
>     withered,
> she stirred the ingredients up and mingled the top with the
>     bottom.
>
> (7.275–78)

"A thousand nameless objects" (275): it's tempting to imagine that Medea begins to take on a life that's independent of her creator here, outrunning Ovid's powers of invention by adding arcane ingredients that, we infer, our poet literally can't name. How to describe exotica that you've never seen before and are beyond your vocabulary? In stirring those ingredients and mixing them up from top to bottom, Medea also stirs and mixes things up in the natural order, and you get the sense that what excites her is more the process than the outcome. After the elaborate preparations, the rejuvenation is briefly recounted in just nine lines of matter-of-fact description, as if for Medea the thrill lies less in the fulfillment than in the invention of her unprecedented concoction. She's already got her eye on her next challenge, it seems, even before Aeson finds himself forty years younger. The true miracle here, perhaps, is that Medea renders Aeson younger even than his own son, Jason.

It was Pelias, Jason's wicked uncle, who sent his nephew on what looked like a suicide mission to get the Golden Fleece in the first place; and that mission would presumably have ended disastrously had Medea not worked her magic to help Jason at every step of the way. There's no sign in Ovid's text that Jason thirsts for revenge against Pelias. By this stage in the Medea saga, he's already begun to look pretty lame and very much like *her* passenger, now that Medea has found her feet after he brought her to Greece. How to make Pelias pay for the virtual death sentence he passed on his nephew? Again, Medea seems less interested in revenge per se than in testing her magical powers yet further. After all, her stated motive for going after Pelias is "so that her deceptions are kept going" (297). The girl who first met Jason was meek; now she's found her mean streak.

The cunning plan: she makes sure that the aged Pelias's daughters hear all about her rejuvenation of Aeson, and they're immediately won over; can Medea do the same for Pelias? Consummate actress that she is, Medea milks the moment: first a dramatic pause as if to consider the matter before she eventually consents to work her magic for Pelias, and then a showy practice run in turning a clapped-out ram back into a lamb. But it's not enough now for Medea just to reprise her rejuvenation trick. Pelias's daughters want her to repeat her magic, but Medea's ceaseless appetite for moreness forbids mere repetition. Hence her exquisite new gambit: she kills with words, not potions, in that she persuades Pelias's daughters to empty their father's veins by cutting into them in advance (they think!) of a transfusion of rejuvenating elixir. Medea paradoxically murders Pelias without being the actual murderer; she achieves a magical result by *not* applying any true magic; and she turns the daughters' act of devotion to their father into an act of parricide. When she plunges her own knife into Pelias's neck to finish him off once and for all, it's just the slicing on the cake.

Still Medea strives for more. After arriving in Corinth, she tweaks her technique of inducing Pelias's daughters to kill their father, this time by experimenting with another murder weapon: she has her own children deliver to the Greek princess who's usurped her marriage bed the poisoned robe that will kill her; and yet worse is to follow when she murders those same children and then almost succeeds in deploying Aegeus to kill his own flesh and blood in the form of Theseus. All in all, the metamorphic thrust of her story lies not just or so much in the transformations she brings about in rejuvenating Aeson, say, or in turning Pelias's loyal daughters into parricides. She too undergoes a gradual process of change into an increasingly shrewd if shameless and ruthless operator—an adept dramaturge and actress who specializes in ever more complex and macabre theatricalities. But then an arresting development: as she makes her escape from Pelias's palace en route for Corinth, she takes wing on a freewheeling tour of the Aegean before turning back to the Greek mainland. Along the way, it's as if to fly with Medea, or to follow her flight path, is to see metamorphic wonder everywhere as she surveys the landscape below her at her cruising altitude of five thousand feet: no fewer than fifteen arcane stories of metamorphosis are associated with the places she passes over. Her whole itinerary is a learned literary compendium of sorts—a kind of composition on the fly, and with several points of contact with stories that Ovid tells within the *Metamorphoses* at large.

What to make of this metamorphic fabric that takes shape as Medea wings it above the Aegean? Here, unfolding before our eyes, is her most audacious undertaking yet: in the fifteen tales of change, Medea's journey suggestively offers an alternative vision or microversion of the fifteen-book *Metamorphoses* itself—even a sort of *Medeamorphoses* that muscles in on Ovid's macropoem. Already in book 6 two stories are told of sublime artists—the weaver Arachne and the piper Marsyas—who dare to challenge the gods to contests in their respective skills, and both are harshly punished when they're promptly vanquished. We've already observed Medea's competitive instinct. But does she now outdo the likes of Arachne and Marsyas in the previous book by mounting an extraordinary artistic challenge of her own—a surreal assault on Ovid's authorial control of the very poem in which he tells her life story? If we push harder in this direction, what we find is a Medea who is not just adept at making rivers run backward through her magic, controlling the motions of the winds, clouds, and seas, and drawing down the moon (199–209); she also seems dangerously capable of diverting the entire flow of Ovid's *Metamorphoses*. He terms his poem a *carmen* (1.4), but that Latin word can also denote a magical spell, as it does when it occurs in the Medea episode: magical *carmen* competes against Ovidian *carmen* as Medea infiltrates the heart of the *Metamorphoses*, as if a usurper within.

Medea almost gets away with murdering Theseus through the agency of Aegeus, but for once a happy accident prevents disaster in the *Metamorphoses*: Aegeus recognizes Theseus as his son before it's too late, and Medea is at last thwarted. She's developed into a dynamo of empowered womanhood through the growth phases of Ovid's biography of her in book 7, but enough is enough: as we imagine her flying off into the metaspace of her continuing travels beyond the confines of the *Metamorphoses*, we're left to speculate on where she'll land next, what evil she'll perpetrate when she gets there, and how her endless appetite for moreness can ever be satisfied. She disappears from the poem, but the unnerving point is that she does so as a still dangerously potent force who changes all she touches. Ovid has left us to invent the script of her next adventures, as if her greatest magic is to cause us to devise imagined narratives that can live up to her legend: what a creation! She's a world away from the far more ordinary-looking Medea in Paulus Bor's rendering of her in figure 2: if Bor captures the banality of despairing disillusionment before Medea's terrible act of infanticide, Ovid has gone to the opposite extreme by hyperactivating his archvillainess.

## Gender Change: The Cases of Iphis and Hermaphroditus

Ovid's Medea well illustrates the complexity of gender identity in the *Metamorphoses* even before we focus on literal gender change elsewhere in the poem. After arriving as Jason's bride in Greece, she's a committed wife who rejuvenates his father, Aeson; and after Jason abandons her and she takes her terrible revenge against him and his new bride, she goes on to marry Aegeus, as we've seen. But even as she marries and remarries in the traditional fashion, she appears to outgrow any ordinary categories of gender definition. It's not so much that she's male-like in her steely aggression. Rather, she evolves from a maiden who falls in love into a woman who begins to channel her passions differently, with little or no sign of any lingering erotic spark or sexual impulse. The Medea who reorders nature seems to do so even in the case of her own nature: she grows into a superhuman figure of indeterminate identity—a sort of non-gendered and postsexual singularity in the *Metamorphoses*.

Literal cases of gender change are a different matter and are numerous enough in the poem to constitute a metamorphic subgenre of their own. From a modern perspective, one of the most arresting stories is that of Iphis in book 9. Born a girl but

Figure 2. Paulus Bor, *The Disillusioned Medea*, c. 1640.

*Source*: Art Resource, NY. Copyright the Metropolitan Museum of Art, New York.

brought up as a boy, Iphis is set to marry the beautiful Ianthe and is transformed by the Egyptian goddess Isis (in a Roman context, another exotic touch) from female to male so that the union can be consummated. This story offers an important provocation in a twenty-first-century context where gender is fluid and definable by how we choose to self-identify. To the modern eye, the happy ending of the Iphis story may at first imply a moment of progressive Ovidian editorializing: an openness to the mutability of gendered experience and a form of sexual deregulation in times when the emperor Augustus was using moral legislation to regulate Roman sexual *mores* (as we saw in the introduction). Despite the happy outcome, however, the tale is riddled with unsettling ambiguities.

To begin with, Iphis's metamorphosis into a male magically facilitates the socially sanctioned validation of a same-sex union that Iphis herself views as unnatural. Hence she agonizes in soliloquy over her love for Ianthe:

> Cows never burn with desire for cows, nor mares for
> mares;
> ewes are attracted to rams and every stag has his hind;
> the same with the mating of birds. Throughout the animal
> kingdom
> the female is never smitten with passionate love for a
> female.
> I wish I had never been born a woman, I wish I were dead!
>
> (9.731–35)

Male transformation enables her to fulfill her desire. But that transformation in a sense changes nothing because Iphis is transmuted into the male that Ianthe had always thought her to be. Further, Iphis's father had insisted that, if his wife, Telethusa, bore a girl, the baby would have to be killed. This was a grim but not uncommon reality in the ancient world, where a male child (as labor in waiting) was less of a financial liability than a girl, not least because of the pressure of providing a dowry as and when she married. Against this background, Iphis ends up as the son her father had prayed for, and when the happy couple ties the knot as husband and wife, the open-church feel of the same-sex storyline arguably reverts to a safe resolution in heterosexual normativity. Is this an edgy story celebrating the triumph of sexual otherness or one that backslides into conventionality?

Then there's the tension between biological sex and performative gender, with the added effect of environmental shaping. Iphis is Cretan, and she's quick to wonder if her sexual otherness is conditioned by context: "Crete is the land of every perversion," she declares (736), in that Pasiphaë, another Cretan, notoriously produced the Minotaur after mating with a bull. Iphis suspects that she outdoes even Pasiphaë in deviating from what's normal, but what comes under increasing scrutiny in this episode is just what normativity is or should be. On this approach, Iphis was born into her "normal" Cretan nature, and her name, originally her grandfather's name, "was common / to either sex and meant [Iphis's mother] could use it without deceit" (709–10). Boy/girl by name, she was also always boy/girl by appearance, lovely from either perspective (712–13): what her story ultimately symbolizes, perhaps, is not so much the slipperiness of gender categories or mobility between them but the inadequacy of socially and culturally defined markers of such difference. Lives, modern as well as ancient, are so much more complex than the classificatory categories that too often sort and systematize them. The biological assignment of gender at birth may be one thing; how gender is perceived, constructed, or channeled at a societal level is quite another—a cultural insight that Ovid captures acutely and with important resonances in modern-day reflection on the instability of gender and the language of gender definition.

Ovid's first extended treatment of gender change, or (better in this case) gender fusion, occurs in the story of Salmacis and Hermaphroditus in book 4. This tale offers a good example of how the spectacle of gender change itself, however sensationally described by Ovid, is often only the culmination of a process of change that evolves more gradually in a given storyline. The physical change grabs the headlines, but of greater interest for now are the literary, psychological, or circumstantial factors that set change in motion, or motivate the change, well before the climactic transformation happens. To develop this point, let's consider the fuller context for Ovid's account of how Hermaphroditus truly grew into his name by becoming a hermaphrodite.

The story so far goes like this. The god Bacchus comes to Thebes, destroying its ruler Pentheus and bringing the city under his intoxicating sway. The only lingering resistance comes from the daughters of one Minyas, three sisters who refuse to take part in the general revels that greet Bacchus's arrival. A festival day is held in the god's honor, but the sisters stay away, engaging instead in spinning and weaving in their steadfast devotion to Minerva, the goddess of handicrafts. To while away the time as they spin the yarn, the sisters all spin yarns, each of them erotic in thrust, and a metamorphosis features in all three.

The first of the stories is the tragic tale of the ill-starred lovers Pyramus and Thisbe, a sort of Ovidian Romeo and Juliet: after they elope, both end up committing suicide after Pyramus wrongly infers, because of a sequence of grimly absurd misunderstandings, that Thisbe is dead; thereafter, as a monument to their forbidden love, the fruit of the mulberry tree is transformed from white to the mournful hue of dark purple. The second sister, Leuconoë, then tells how Mars and Venus were caught in bed together by Venus's husband Vulcan, entrapped there by him, and exposed to the ridicule of the gods. It was the Sun who informed Vulcan of the affair, and so the Sun gets his comeuppance when Venus sees to it that his passion for a new heartthrob, Leucothoë, ends badly. Leucothoë is metamorphosed into a frankincense shrub, and another character, Clytië, the Sun's jealous ex-lover, is turned into a heliotrope. The reaction to this story is telling:

> Leuconoë finished. Her wonderful tale had entranced her
> audience.
> Some said, "It couldn't have happened"; but others
> declared, "Real gods
> can do anything!"—Bacchus, however, was not included
> among them.

> (4.271–73)

With this breezy dismissal of Bacchus as a "real god," the stage is set for the third story. It's told by Alcithoë, who is introduced at the start of book 4 as something of a ringleader in her dismissal of Bacchus's divine credentials:

> Only a handful of women rejected the revels of Bacchus.
> One was Alcithoë, Minyas' daughter, foolhardy enough
> to deny that the god was Jupiter's son; and her impious sisters
> shared this wicked belief.
>
> (4.1–4)

In rejecting love stories that are "too well known" (276), Alcithoë showily chooses a more obscure path. Even a story that's attested nowhere else apart from here in Ovid gets rejected:

> Nor shall I tell how once, in breach of the laws of nature,
> Sithon's gender could alternate between male and female.
>
> (4.279–80)

Sithon's story is laid aside, but Alcithoë remains keen to persist at least with the theme of gender change. Hence she focuses on the notorious fountain of Salmacis in Caria in Asia Minor: why is it that males who bathe in its waters are apparently effeminized by the experience?

Salmacis is a nymph synonymous with the fountain, and here the trouble starts. She sees the fifteen-year-old Hermaphroditus, beautiful and innocent, and she's consumed with lust for him. He rejects her, she backs off, but she hangs about in the nearby bushes, and when he strips off to bathe in the water, it's all too much for her. He jumps in, and she goes in after him, seizing him in an embrace from which he can't escape. She prays to the gods to "decree / that the day never comes when the two of us here shall be riven asunder!" (371–72). Apparently without pity for the boy, the gods grant her prayer, but with a twist: if Salmacis meant endless sexual union, they interpret her words far more literally. The two bodies become one, a fusion of male and female so perfectly melded that "they seemed to be neither and both" (379). Hermaphroditus is first named in the episode only after this fusion takes place. Hermaphroditus may have been his name from birth, but he's at last transformed into the true essence of his name. The metamorphosis is in a sense from the upper case to the lower: from being Hermaphroditus by descent from Hermes (Mercury) and Aphrodite (Venus), he becomes a hermaphrodite through the seamless merging of boy and girl.

The story is cleverly told by Alcithoë, but there's something funny going on. After the tragic tale of Pyramus and Thisbe, the second sister's account of Mars's affair with Venus and of the Sun's lust for Leucothoë takes things in a sexually charged direction before Alcithoë goes a stage further: full-blown nymphomania and titillating gender fusion in the case of Salmacis and Hermaphroditus. The story of Pyramus and Thisbe is set in Babylon, that of the Sun and Leucothoë in Persia, and the Salmacis tale in Lycia in Asia Minor: there's an exotic, eastern accent to all three tales—an intriguing development so soon after that charismatic infiltrator from the East, Bacchus, has taken over Thebes, loosening minds and *mores* as he does so. Then consider what unfolds between Salmacis and Hermaphroditus: the genders are blended and confused even before our two main protagonists become one. So far in the *Metamorphoses* nymphs like Salmacis are the prey of divine rapists such as Apollo and Jupiter, and flower picking is a prime moment of vulnerability when young maidens tend to catch the eye of the predatory gods. But when Salmacis is shown picking flowers, it's just before she catches sight of Hermaphroditus and plays the predator; it's she who here takes on the aggressive male role. She's also Narcissus-like as she gazes into the mirrorlike waters and pampers herself before her own reflection. And when she first addresses Hermaphroditus, her sexually freighted words of seduction are inflected with echoes of Odysseus's words to the young princess Nausicaä when he's washed up on the island of Phaeacia in the *Odyssey*; whereas the shipwrecked Odysseus is stark naked and straining to hide his modesty before the maidenly princess, Salmacis is desperate to get naked and flaunt her immodesty. By contrast, in his sexual innocence Hermaphroditus resembles the virginal nymphs who are so often exploited in the *Metamorphoses*: when Salmacis makes her advances, he blushes because "he didn't know what love was" (329–30). He's a she and she's a he in a shared crossover of their genders even before they're conjoined as a hermaphroditic unity.

But now Bacchus casts a shadow over the proceedings. He too has a certain hermaphroditic quality to him. Late in book 3 he's said to be "a boy with a beautiful face like a girl's" (607). Early in book 4 he's heralded as having "the comeliest form / of all the gods on Olympus, a face . . . / fair as a virgin girl's" (18–20). Alcithoë brashly refuses to acknowledge Bacchus's divinity, we remember: does she tell her story of Salmacis and Hermaphroditus with irreverent sarcasm, as if none-too-subtly casting Bacchus as an effeminized imposter of a god? Perhaps. But let's not underestimate Bacchus's resilience, especially after his effortless destruction of the god-baiting Pentheus in book 3. Pentheus thinks he has the upper hand in controlling the spread of the Bacchic pandemic, only to die horrifically when he's torn limb from limb by the god's infatuated devotees, Pentheus's own mother among them. He disastrously underestimated the god's capacity to infiltrate minds, perhaps his own included: when Pentheus goes to Mount Cithaeron to witness for himself those crazed devotees in action, it's hard not to suspect that, for all his ostensible anger, they turn him on before they turn on him (3.701–7).

Then we should bear in mind Bacchus's other exploit in book 3: hijacked by pirates at sea, the god stymies his captors by tangling their oars with ivy and bedecking their sails with its tendrils so that the boat is brought to a standstill; soon after, the pirates are transformed into dolphins that plunge into the water. It's important to keep an eye on the ivy in the larger Bacchus sequence in books 3 and 4. When Alcithoë's story is finished in book 4, the three sisters' looms grow green, and their weavings are changed into "leafy curtains of ivy" (395): the process of their punishment has begun, and it's completed when Bacchus turns them into bats. But then consider a detail in the Salmacis story: entrapping Hermaphroditus in the pool that bears her name, she grips him "like the ivy which weaves its way round the length of a tree-trunk" (365)—the telltale sign of Bacchic vengeance!

At last the realization dawns: in its racy subject matter, Alcithoë's story is already, whether she knows it or not, going in a Bacchic direction; what she offers is a raunchier, still more unfettered advance on the two stories told so far by her sisters in book 4. Further, Alcithoë's account centers on the tension between exuberant sexual release on the one hand and resistance to it on the other: Salmacis propositions Hermaphroditus and the boy holds back, but he's inevitably ensnared in the end, as if caught up in the (Bacchic-like!) ivy tendrils to which Salmacis's grip is compared. From this angle, Alcithoë's story of aggressive seduction and stubborn aversion offers a powerful allegory of sorts for the battle of wills in book 3 between Bacchus and Pentheus, or between the God of Liberation and the King of Containment.

It may not have been quite right, then, to suspect earlier on that Alcithoë rejects love stories that "are too well known" (4.276) largely because she wants to show off her learning by telling the obscure tale of Salmacis. A different or additional possibility now beckons, and it involves mind games: was Alcithoë influenced all along by the creeping effects of Bacchus, that seductive intoxicator who works on the daughters of Minyas even as they imagine they're capable of resisting his magnetism? At the end of the episode, Ovid makes an abrupt transition to their metamorphosis into bats:

> Alcithoë's story was ended, and still the daughters of
>     Minyas
> kept at their weaving in scorn of Bacchus, profaning his
>     feast day.
> Suddenly, out of nowhere, their ears were harshly assaulted
> by clattering drums, the fearful skirling of Phrygian pipes
> and the strident clashing of cymbals.
>
> (4.389–93)

There's no stopping the Bacchic din as it suddenly fills the sisters' chamber and overwhelms the place. But all that noise shouldn't distract us from the quieter inference: Alcithoë may have been the ringleader of the sisters' resistance to the god, but the traces of Bacchus in her story already indicate that she's testing positive for Bacchic infiltration even before she's turned into a bat. The Hermaphroditus story is no stand-alone extravaganza in this respect, as if an Ovidian set piece that explores gender change for its own sake. It's vitally conditioned by its contextual setting, with Alcithoë inadvertently channeling Bacchus even as she means to disavow him.

Like the Bacchic ivy that spreads its tendrils to devastating effect, then, the entire Bacchus sequence in books 3 and 4 as a whole has far-reaching effects on the Hermaphroditus episode. Salmacis and Hermaphroditus are colorful characters in their own right, and still more so when they're conjoined as one. But the daughters of Minyas are also key players here, Alcithoë above all, especially if we suspect that she's been stealthily overtaken by Bacchus's influence. The god first enters the *Metamorphoses* in book 3 when he's retrieved from Semele's womb after she's blasted by Jupiter's bolt, as we saw earlier in this chapter; after her demise, Jupiter sewed her unborn son into his thigh so as to complete the process of gestation. When Bacchus comes of age and into his own in books 3 and 4, he effortlessly captivates Pentheus's Thebes. But what about his symbolic potential as he begins to make his mark in Ovid's world of change—not just actively present in many episodes but also as a dynamic essence at a more intuitive level within the text? After all, Bacchus was hailed in Greco-Roman antiquity as the god of wine and, by extension, as the inspirer of music and poetry. Many characters in the *Metamorphoses* embark on voyages of self-discovery, and they often release their inner urges, capacities, yearnings, and proclivities along the way: can we detect in

Bacchus's lingering presence in the poem a symbol of this eman-
cipatory impulse? We saw how Medea was ultimately foiled in
her effort to hijack the *Metamorphoses* in book 7, but now a different force perhaps has to be reckoned with: if Bacchus is seen
to begin infiltrating the *Metamorphoses* in book 3, as if a metaphor for spiritual and sexual emancipation within the poem,
Ovid has *already* explored the idea of literary usurpation
even before Medea launches her hostile takeover bid just a few
books later.

# 2

## The Liabilities of Language

### Change and Instability in Ovid's World of Words

W here to turn for reliable information about the world around us? And how to navigate a world in which fake news appears so prevalent? "Fake news" was declared the *Collins Dictionary* Word of the Year for 2017 in recognition of a phenomenon that was hardly new but freshly energized by— and soon synonymous with—the U.S. presidency of Donald Trump. Already in an ancient Roman context, an article on fake news in the British *Daily Telegraph* of January 7, 2021, had this to say: "Octavian famously used a campaign of disinformation to aid his victory over Marc Antony in the final war of the Roman Republic. In its aftermath, he changed his name to Augustus, and dispatched a flattering and youthful image of himself throughout the Empire, maintaining its use in his old age."

In many ways, Augustus was a composer in his own right, the author of a carefully regulated script of governance in which controlling the message was all; and countless other examples could of course be cited from many ages and cultures of ruling elites whose authority, prestige, and even survival owed (and still owe) so much to image projection and manipulation.

But even if the phenomenon of fake news is now old news, the rise of the internet and social media has given it a potency and reach that were unthinkable only three or so decades ago. For all the benefits brought by the marvel of the web, and for all the positive effects of social media as a means of connecting us with one another, the truth nowadays serially competes with image projection, makeover, hearsay, distortion, and flat-out fabrication in the information flowing to our phones and iPads. Then we tune into the Fox News Channel, CNN, MSNBC, CBS: the same news items, but different spins, different agendas, different talking heads. How to find and fix the truth as we surf the channels?

Many of the challenges posed by our experience of the world as mediated through social media, news media, and Google searches—the need to sift fact from possible fiction, to be wary of layered versions of reality, to sense the hidden agenda underlying surface dissimulation—are already embedded in the *Metamorphoses*. The first chapter explored what we termed Ovid's explosion of characterful diversity and individuality in his poem of change: it pulses with an ever-shifting cast of quirky, engaging, sympathetic or repulsive personalities, many of whom grow and evolve transformatively before our eyes even before they undergo physical metamorphosis. But in this chapter we turn to the changefulness that is rooted in language itself in the *Metamorphoses*.

Beyond the physical transformations that happen within Ovid's stories, change is fundamental to his plotlines because sudden shifts of speaker disrupt narrative continuity, different voices express themselves with all sorts of private motivations, and the "truth" they deliver is so often open to qualification, skepticism, or downright rejection. Of course, other Roman poets are clearly adept at the kind of voice control and truth manipulation that Ovid shows. In combination with his sublime abilities as a wordsmith, however, what sets Ovid apart is the particular set of sociocultural circumstances and provocations that prevailed when he penned the *Metamorphoses* between 2 and 8 CE.

The date of composition matters because of the changing atmospherics of Augustus's Rome in the last decade or so of his reign before his death in 14 CE. The times were unsettling. The saga of who would eventually succeed Augustus was resolved only in 4 CE when, as something of a last resort, he had little choice but to designate his stepson, Tiberius, as his heir. There was scandal in the imperial house through the sexual intrigues of the two Julias, Augustus's daughter and granddaughter; they both ended up in exile. Then there were the long-term trickledown effects of disquiet at Augustus's moral reforms; there were conspiracies against him, military disasters abroad, and bouts of famine at home. These and other factors all contributed to the rising tide of intolerance that's visible in and around 4 CE. Even if the scale and severity of that intolerance should not be overestimated (as we saw in the introduction), the basic fact of it holds good: in those later years, Augustus's power hardened in the direction of monarchy, and in that climate Ovid's brand of playful, even subversive provocation in his *Art of Love* was asking for trouble even before his *Metamorphoses* and *Fasti* (an elegiac poem on the Roman calendar that survives in six of twelve projected books) showcased his eye for irreverent flamboyance yet further.

But despite this provocative side, Ovid's exquisite control of language also captures the climate of caution and qualification in which the *Metamorphoses* was written. The work offers many examples of outspokenness punished and loose tongues suppressed. Short of keeping your mouth shut, better to proceed with ambiguity and suggestion; in that way you can convey your guarded meaning to those in the know without risking offense to the powers that be. On other occasions, Ovid's characters seek to mislead or manipulate their listeners for selfish or playful ends, to persuade them of one thing or dissuade them from believing another, and they pitch their voices and modulate their words accordingly. Hence the form of linguistic changefulness that concerns us in this chapter: the words Ovid voices through his colorful speakers are often shifting and unstable in the ambiguities they generate and the mixed messages they send according to the perspective from which they're read and understood. The challenge for the reader is frequently to avoid being beguiled by the slipperiness of meanings, to tell truth from falsehood, and to decipher what a person is really saying and why. Indeed, shouldn't we expect language itself to go the way of all things in the *Metamorphoses*—to be caught up, that is, in the existential flux that the poem describes? On this approach the poem offers a precious resource, we might say, in sensitizing us to the dangers of layered speech, message manipulation, and plausible fiction in the internet age: a poem of our times.

Let's start with two examples of this linguistic slipperiness in action, both of them with major implications for how we read the *Metamorphoses* more generally. The first concerns Ovid's treatment of Augustus. The second features a remarkable moment in book 15 when Ovid comes close to undermining the "philosophy" of metamorphosis that has so far dominated the entire work. We'll then go back to the poem's beginning and set about tracing certain patterns of development in how Ovid treats the dangers, liabilities, and capacities of language from book 1 onward.

## Shifts of Register and Tone: Initial Soundings

Late in book 15, Ovid defers for as long as possible that most momentous metamorphosis of all, Augustus's transformation into a god after his death:

> I call on you, gods who attended Aeneas through fire and
>     sword
> and compelled them to yield; you native Italian gods and
>     Quirinus
> who founded our city; on Mars who fathered unconquered
>     Quirinus;
> Vesta whom Caesar reveres amongst the gods of his
>     household;
> Apollo, an honored neighbor of Caesar as surely as
>     Vesta;
> Jupiter, throned in his temple surmounting the heights of
>     Tarpeia;
> and all of the other gods whom a righteous poet may
>     worship—
> slow to dawn be that day, long after my time, when
>     Augustus
> leaves the world that he rules and rises up to the heavens.
> So may he lend a favouring ear to our prayers from his new
>     home.

(15.861–70)

Aeneas, Quirinus, Mars, Vesta, Apollo, Jupiter: in its invocation of hallowed names and locations, Roman gods and Founding Fathers, this passage heralds a form of arrival and completeness in Augustus. The many names all in a sense converge on him, as if making him synonymous with Rome, its divine destiny, its physical fabric, its past and present: Augustus takes his place here on a verbal Mount Rushmore. But just how easy is it to read Ovid's straight praises with a straight face?

It's now a commonplace in modern scholarship on Ovid to find that he complicates his surface adulation toward the imperial household in book 15 by resorting to irony and innuendo. Here's a good example:

> Of the deeds of Julius Caesar
> none can be greater than that he became the father of
> Caesar Augustus.
> Julius surely could boast that he conquered the islander
> Britons.
> . . . . . . . . . . . . . . . . . . . . . . . . . . . . . . . .
> But how can the glory
> of all these exploits amount to the glory of having begotten
> so glorious a son—a leader, with whom at the head of our
> empire,
> the gods have showered the richest of blessings on all
> mankind?
>
> (15.750–52, 756–59)

Well, let's not forget that Augustus was in fact Julius Caesar's great-nephew and adopted by him in his will (see the introduction); so much for the biological origin implied in "he became the father" (751) and "having begotten" (757). But then a still more compromising touch when, in line 752, Ovid embarks on an impressive list of Julius Caesar's imperial conquests that begin with "the islander Britons." The Latin word for "surely" in 752 is *scilicet*, a term that's unsettling in its ambiguity: does it here underscore a self-evident fact ("Fathering Augustus was *of course* [hear hear!] a greater achievement than conquering the Britons, etc.!")? Or does it sarcastically highlight an obvious absurdity ("*Of course* [ha ha!] it was a greater achievement to have fathered Augustus than to have conquered half the world!")? Nothing is immune to transformation in Ovid's poem of change, not even his praises of Augustus. Read in one way, they laud him to the skies. But change the nuance of *scilicet*, and the same passage suddenly reads very differently, with a message that's far more cynical than sycophantic.

*Of course* Augustus is a worthy successor of Aeneas and Caesar who is specially favored by the Roman pantheon in 15.861–70: a self-evident fact, an obvious absurdity, or somewhere in between? And at what point does high praise in any case risk toppling over into self-undermining hyperbole? But our main concern for now lies not so much with the localized viewpoint or with the intricacies of tone that turn passages like 15.861–70 into an interpretational Rubik's cube. Rather, the poem as a whole has repeatedly taught us to take little or nothing at face value, so that when we finally arrive at Ovid's praises of the House of Windsor in book 15, his rendition of the national anthem is already cursed by context. This destabilizing effect is well illustrated by the episode that largely dominates the first half of book 15 before Ovid rises to his climax in Augustus: an eccentric discourse offered by the semilegendary Greek philosopher and mystic Pythagoras.

Pythagoras is introduced in book 15 when Numa, later the second king of Rome after Romulus, travels to the southern Italian town of Croton to seek instruction about the nature of the universe. There a local elder tells the story of how Pythagoras came to live in Croton, and he goes on to deliver in Pythagoras's reported voice a rambling speech that extends for over four hundred lines. After all the tales of change that have been recounted so far in the poem, change itself is theorized as a basic principle of nature in this exhaustive (and exhausting) exposition. Pythagoras's presence here is itself disconcerting, as if taking the poem in an unexpected direction just when we're getting ready for Ovid to rise to his finale in the Now of Augustus's Rome. But the substance of Pythagoras's speech is still more disconcerting. Fundamental to his doctrine are the transmigration of the soul and its reincarnation in a new body after death; hence his advocacy of vegetarianism, as meat-eaters risk devouring their own reincarnated relatives. This discourse poses major challenges for our understanding of the poem as a whole. Beyond the difficulty of gauging its tone (is it a serious intellectual experiment or a spoof?), how, if at all, is its theme of transmigration to be reconciled with the phenomenon of metamorphosis as experienced in the previous fourteen books?

One possibility is that Ovid offers through Pythagoras some kind of philosophical underpinning for the dynamic of changefulness in the world of the *Metamorphoses*. After all, the theory of soul migration is couched in Ovid's language of change:

All is subject to change and nothing to death. The spirit
in each of us wanders from place to place; it enters whatever

body it pleases, crossing over from beast to man,
and back again to a beast. It never perishes wholly.

(15.165–68)

But then a shocking afterthought that changes everything: does Ovid jeopardize a fundamental premise of his work by propagating, almost at the poem's end, a theory of *ongoing* change? Reincarnation of the Pythagorean kind presupposes a continuous state of metamorphosis from life to life, body to body, but in Ovid metamorphosis brings about a single, permanent transformation: if Pythagoras is right, Ovid's got it all wrong. The *Metamorphoses* appears to be on life support at this point, as if drained of meaning; but there may yet be a saving grace. This is how Pythagoras's discourse is introduced:

His audiences listened in wondering
silence while he explained how the universe first began,
discoursed at length upon causes, defined what Nature and
    God were.
. . . . . . . . . . . . . . . . . . . . . . . . . . . . . .
This sage was the first to condemn
the consumption of animal food and the first to express
    such a doctrine,
*informed as it was but not given credit*, in words such as these.

(15.66–68, 72–74)

According to Ovid, or rather the local elder of Croton who reports Pythagoras's speech early in book 15 (but can we really trust that elder?), Pythagoras was heard attentively enough, *but he wasn't believed.* An incidental detail, it may at first appear, but in retrospect it proves hugely significant: Pythagoras's doctrine might just have destabilized the entirety of the *Metamorphoses*, if only his words had convinced his audience. That preannounced failure to persuade before Pythagoras gets going vindicates Ovid's different take on one-time metamorphosis, it seems, and we can rest easy once more. But what if we then succumb to yet another nagging doubt? Pythagoras may not have been believed, but the fact you're not believed doesn't necessarily mean you're wrong: was he right all along, as if a Cassandra-like truth teller who deserved more credit than he got? If so, has Ovid indeed short-circuited his own greatest creation by fatally undermining his own theory of one-time metamorphosis?

By the time we reach Ovid's celebration of Augustus at the end of book 15, then, the Pythagoras episode majestically confirms all the insecurities that our larger engagement with the poem has already generated in us. His praises of the Royal Family are difficult to take at face value precisely because a flat, one-dimensional reading of them can't sustain itself after all the degrees of fiction, distortion, and fake news that bedevil the first fourteen-and-a-half books. Let's now take samplings from this rogue's gallery earlier in the poem—an ominously shaky foundation for the House of Augustus as built in book 15.

## Controlling the Narrative

The first major episode of the *Metamorphoses* recounts the Creation and the birth of mortals and then humankind's degeneration from Golden Age innocence to Iron Age corruption. Isn't it a little disconcerting to encounter this negative transformation just as Ovid's poem of change is getting going? To begin at the very beginning, however: the feature of the Creation that matters most for now is the first stirring of sound as the world takes shape. Let's listen carefully as the unnamed creator god gets to work, separating out the elements (fire, air, water, earth), positioning Earth's sphere so that it hangs in the middle of the cosmos, and partitioning the seas and the lands and the different climatic zones.

What sounds can we hear or imagine as the god imposes his commands (*iussit* three times in the Latin) and forces obedience on the winds and waters? Those howling winds

> can scarcely
> be stopped from tearing the world to pieces, though each
>     of them governs
> his blasts in a distant quarter; so angrily brothers can quarrel.
>
> (1.58–60)

In Ovid's Latin, their clashing and crashing assault our ears, as when "Boreas, lord of the blizzard, sweeps / into Scythia, land of the frozen north" (64–65). A snappy translation, but not nearly as cacophonous as the raging sibilance of the Latin: *Scythiam septemque Triones/ horrifer invasit Boreas.* Loud thunderclaps are added to the mix "to trouble the hearts of men" (55). After the quiet serenity of the Golden Age, the Silver and Bronze Ages bring more strident times:

> The sky for the first time burned and glowed with a dry
>     white heat,

and the blasts of the wild winds froze the rain into
    hanging icicles.

(1.119–20)

You can hear the boiling effects of the seething heat of line 119 in the hissing *s*-sounds of the Latin (***siccis aer fervoribus ustus***), only for the harsh *t-* and *c-* crackle of cold suddenly to take over in line 120 (***ventis glacies astricta pependit***); the juxtaposition of hot and cold in the two lines is itself disquieting in its contrariness. As hard toil begins to take its toll, all we hear is weariness ("oxen *groaned*beneath the weight of the heavy yoke" [124]). Finally, the Iron Age corrodes and corrupts language itself:

> Loyalty, truth and conscience
> went into exile, their throne usurped by guile and deception,
> treacherous plots, brute force and a criminal lust for
>     possession.

(1.129–31)

No wonder that—apart from the creator god's ordering voice (*iussit* three times) as he assigns the world-parts to their places—the first vocal expression reported of a human or divine character in the poem is Jupiter's groan (*ingemit* [164]) at the sins of Lycaön, the wicked king of Arcadia. On a visit to Arcadia Jupiter had been outraged by Lycaön's impious rejection of his divinity. After attempting to murder the god in his sleep, Lycaön had tried to test Jupiter's true identity by serving him a taboo meal of human flesh. Lycaön is in fact the first mortal named in the poem (hardly an encouraging introduction to humankind!), and Ovid causes our ears to prick up when we hear his name: "Wolfman" by derivation from Greek λύκος/*lukos*, Lycaön finally gets his comeuppance when he's transformed into a wolf, as if at last inhabiting his own true nature. Jupiter's anger rages loudly, he "give[s] vent to his wrath" (181) when he convenes a crisis meeting of the gods, and there's uproar when the assembled divinities hear all about Lycaön's outrages—only for Jupiter to provoke mixed murmurings in his audience when he decides to punish the entirety of the human race for the excesses of Lycaön alone.

For all the care with which Ovid orchestrates this Creation, what we hear is a confusion of inarticulate noisiness as the world (and the *Metamorphoses*) begins to take shape. This primal disharmony has important implications for the fifteen-book arc of the poem and for Ovid's smooth articulation at the end of book 15 of Augustus's place as the divinely ordained successor of Aeneas and Julius Caesar. As we saw in the introduction, already in the prologue to book 1 Ovid prays for a steady path of evolution in the work as he proceeds "from the world's beginning / down to my own lifetime" (3–4). A continuous thread leads from the raw soundscape of the Beginning to the distilled fluency with which he finally delivers his praises of Augustus and the First Family in book 15. The poem progresses from a chaos of noise in book 1, we might say, to an apex of "finished" and fawning Augustan wording at its finale. But so much for this clean model of A-to-Z linearity that nicely fits with Ovid's opening vision of "one continuous poem" (1.4). Things quickly become complicated when Ovid gets into his stride after the Creation and the poem begins to meander in its twist-and-turn sequence of often tangentially related episodes.

The unnamed creator god who shapes the world early in book 1 offers a tempting analogy for Ovid as the architect of his own literary cosmos in the *Metamorphoses*. Both god and poet order their respective worlds with a clinical efficiency; but things are very different not just for Ovid's dazzled readership but also for many of the characters who populate his episodes. The challenge for the reader is to keep track of the kaleidoscopic cascade of storylines that begins after the Creation and to make sense of the linkages and sudden leaps between them; and then to be wary of the ulterior motives and self-interested agendas that quietly inflect countless characters' words and actions. As for the characters themselves, they're often shown struggling to seize or maintain control of dramatic situations, to hold their audiences, or to advance their own special interests—a picture complicated by the frequently tangled or colliding motivations of competing players in a given scene.

Some characters control their words well, some don't, and we'll sample both sides of the picture from two viewpoints. First, in the next section of this chapter, a form of unconscious self-betrayal occupies a special linguistic niche of its own in the *Metamorphoses*: if we listen carefully enough, many characters inadvertently reveal their true natures in the words they spin and/or imperfectly control; they can't see, limit, or back away from the full implications of what they say, often to self-defeating effect. Second, in the penultimate section, there are the self-serving wheeler-dealers who are naturals in manipulative speech and should therefore put us on our guard. Our star illustration in the first category is Apollo, in a passage a little after the midpoint of book 1. The legendary Greek hero Nestor stars in the second category, in a passage from book 12. As we'll see, Apollo's clumsiness with words is at odds with Nestor's meticulous control of language, fakery, and the reported "truth." This difference suggests that, at least in the startup phase of the poem, the art of speech is itself finding its way and has yet to mature into the kind of worldliness that's more visible in later books. But let's let Ovid's Apollo—the god of music and poetry, no less—speak ineptly for himself when he falls in love in book 1.

## Apollo and Daphne: A Running Commentary

Not a very reassuring pair: if we're already perturbed by Jupiter's highhanded punishment (via a catastrophic flood) of all humankind in connection with the Lycaön business earlier in book 1, Apollo hardly cuts an impressive figure when we first encounter him later in the book. We can only hope (against hope?) that, as the *Metamorphoses* hurries on, these pillars of the pantheon are transformed into rather more august representatives of divine decorum; and if we do our best to begin reading the poem as loyal supporters of Augustus, just how uplifting is it to recall the special affiliation that Augustus claimed with both Apollo and Jupiter? But to look on the brighter side for now, Apollo first battles the monstrous Python before the Daphne episode begins:

> Sprawling over Parnassus, it horribly frightened the
>     new-born
> peoples, until it was killed by the deadly shafts of Apollo,
> whose only targets before were the timid gazelles and the
>     roe deer.
> The snake was transfixed by a thousand arrows (the quiver
>     was almost

emptied) and out of its wounds there spewed black gushes
   of venom.
In order that time should never destroy the fame of this
   exploit,
Apollo established the sacred games, attended by huge
   crowds,
the Pythian Games, called after the serpent he
   vanquished, Python.

(1.440–47)

Mythology meets history in the origin Ovid claims here for the
Pythian Games, the athletic and musical festival that was held
every four years at Delphi from the early sixth century BCE
onward. Apollo is transformed from a boyish hunter of "the
timid gazelles and the roe deer" (442) into a serpent-slaying
warrior—but just how skilled a shooter is he really? After all,
would William Tell need a quiver big enough to hold a thousand shafts, and how many would he have used to destroy the
Python? For all his tough-nut claim to glory (Ovid writes a
good minispoof here of epic heroism in battle), there's a heavy-
handed quality to Apollo's exploit, with implications that only
become apparent when we move on to Ovid's next story: Apollo's pursuit of the nymph Daphne and her transformation into a
laurel tree to escape his clutches. Victors at the Pythian Games
were awarded the laurel wreath that was sacred to Apollo. Hence
the Daphne story explains that sacred association: "Since you
[Daphne] cannot be mine in wedlock," cries Apollo at the end
of his chase (557–59), "you must at least be Apollo's tree. It is
you who will always / be twined in my hair, on my tuneful lyre
and my quiver of arrows."

So how does the Python scene play out in the Daphne episode? After his quiver-sapping slaying of the serpent, Apollo, "still in the flush of his victory" (454), sees the impish Cupid flexing his bow, and he takes him to task for meddling with the weaponry of real warriors such as himself. Apollo is as profligate with words as he is with his shafts. The spray of bullets in the Python scene now gives way to the spray of bombast with which he blasts Cupid, and Apollo appears impervious to the irony that deflates his epic-sized ego: "My numberless arrows have just destroyed the venomous Python," he proclaims (459), as if blind to the virtual confession of trigger-happiness in "numberless." Everything about the Python episode is swollen with overkill, but Cupid is far more clipped in speech and cuter in his tactics. In the language of Roman poetics, Apollo's epic hyperinflation is effortlessly punctured by Cupid's elegy-inflected dart in lines 463–66:

> The son of Venus replied: "Your arrows, Apollo, can shoot
> whatever you choose, but I'll shoot you. As mortal creatures
> must yield to a god, your glory will likewise prove to be
>     subject
> to mine."

In contrast to Apollo's "numberless arrows," Cupid takes just two darts to transform the fortunes not just of the god and Daphne but also of the entire poem. Apollo is shot with a golden shaft that fills him with desire, Daphne with one that's weighted with lead and has the opposite effect. All is set for Apollo's pursuit of his traumatized victim, but Cupid's action here also symbolically implants into the very marrow of the poem an erotic dynamic that remains active throughout the rest of the *Metamorphoses*; it's a virulent strain that's capable of erupting at any time across the books. This erotic dimension fundamentally transforms any pretension the poem still has to being a paid-up epic in the traditional martial sense. It also features a form of sexual violence that is one of the most troubling aspects of the entire *Metamorphoses*—a theme treated in its own right in chapter 4.

Now to the pursuit and to how Apollo's gaucheness reveals itself yet further in the speech he delivers to the terrified Daphne during their high-speed chase. Words mean one thing to him, another to his victim: he may "woo," but she experiences a hostile verbal assault. He "woos" Daphne in words that may seem well organized in one way: is he a diffident beginner ("Apollo's first love was Daphne" [452]) who has studiously pored over a how-to manual, perhaps even Ovid's *Art of Love*? Or does he play the diffident suitor with all the cunning of one practiced in the art of disguising his sleaziness? Cynical or not, he insists that he's a gentle lover with many good qualities. Scared and scarred, she's silenced by terror: it's as if he interprets her unvoiced No! as a teasing Yes that impels him to pursue all the harder. But as Daphne sprints away from him and he tries to keep up, his fast talking is in equal parts self-absorbed ("Now ask who it is that desires you"), cloying ("Have pity!"), wisecracking ("Don't run so fast and I promise to slow down too"), and tin-eared:

> Listen! I am the master of Delphi,
> Claros and Tenedos, Patara's temple too. My father
> is Jupiter. I can reveal the past, the present and future
> to all who seek them. I am the lord of the lyre and song.
>
> (1.515–18)

Daphne, we imagine, is a humble nymph of Thessalian origin who has never needed a passport: has she heard of the hallowed, ego-serving places that Apollo proudly trots out in lines 515–16? He plays the son-of-Jupiter card, but just how dignified does he look as an aggressive, speed-dating namedropper? And how shrewd is it to mention Jupiter when Jupiter's track record as a philanderer was so well established (witness the *Metamorphoses*!) and perhaps known even (or especially, and in warning!) to a nymph who's a devotee of "the virgin goddess Diana" and herself "want[s] to remain a virgin for ever" (476, 486–87)?

Apollo was never going to succeed in his pursuit of Daphne. Cupid's darts had seen to that, making Apollo chase, Daphne desperate to stay chaste. But even if Cupid instigates the pursuit, Apollo chooses his specific words, and he owns his actions in the moment; he couldn't just deny all responsibility when the drug wears off. Beyond the Cupid-induced futility of his gambit, then, he earns our condemnation. This point is underscored when he at last pauses for breath:

> Apollo wanted to say much more, but the terrified Daphne ran all the faster; she left him behind with his speech unfinished.
>
> (1.525–26)

The Latin word for "unfinished" in line 526 is *imperfecta*, a term that can also mean "defective," "flawed," a subsense that has devastating implications here. Quite apart from Cupid's machinations, Apollo's speech is entirely self-defeating; yet he can't see as much through a combination of arrogant divine/male presumption about sexual viability and availability, egotistical blindness, and tonal deafness. When words fail him in this way, he abandons them, but not the pursuit:

> but now the god in his youthful
> ardour was ready no longer to squander his breath on wheedling
> pleas. Spurred on by desire, he followed the trail with new vigour.
>
> (1.530–32)

This redoubled effort changes the tenor of the story, as if a pre-metamorphosis before Daphne is changed into the laurel tree: when Apollo's witless words dry up, the cruel language of predator and prey takes over (533–38), the pursuit is down to pure speed, and Daphne is finally run to ground in a gratuitous moment of Ovidian terror before her transformation.

When Apollo speaks in the Daphne episode, then, his words are as clumsy and excessive as the countless shafts that he sprays at the Python. He's all-knowing in his ability to "reveal the past, the present and future / to all who seek them" (517–18), but he shows a breathtaking lack of self-consciousness in failing to see the ill-directed futility of his speech. Given his starring role in book 1 (but one so ill-starred for Daphne), this Apollo is a trailblazer for vocal insensitivity and incontinence in the poem more generally—in his case, an incontinence that matches his uncontrolled cruelty of action.

Many other examples of this reflex-like "speaking your nature" could be offered, some poignant, others agonizing, and several grimly humorous in their ill-timed delivery. Let's briefly sample two instances of this phenomenon, the first offered by another victim of Apollo, this time with a still more macabre streak of sadism. We briefly touched in the last chapter on the cocky satyr Marsyas: in book 6 he challenges Apollo to a piping contest, and he's promptly defeated. Nothing is said about how the contest was judged, why the verdict went against Marsyas, or whether he really deserved to lose: he just does, however unjustly. Apollo flays him alive in a sequence of lines that really sticks the knife in:

> In spite of his cries, the skin was peeled from his flesh, and
> his body
> was turned into one great wound; the blood was pouring
> all over him,
> muscles were fully exposed, his uncovered veins convulsively
> quivered; the palpitating intestines could well be counted,
> and so could the organs glistening through the wall of his
> chest.
>
> (6.387–91)

"Don't rip me away from myself!" Marsyas cries even as he's being flayed (385). In the Latin, *quid me mihi detrahis?*, the juxtaposed personal pronouns *me* and *mihi* nicely but nastily capture the severance of self as the layers of his skin are peeled apart. The circumstances are horrific, and Marsyas's wordplay at such a moment is shockingly incongruous. But it's a brilliant spark of spontaneous wit nonetheless, as if what the scalpel exposes isn't just Marsyas's innards but also his inner nature.

After Marsyas's exquisitely painful quip, a more poignant instance of "speaking your nature" occurs in a famous passage of book 8. Daedalus, the Thomas Edison of his mythical times, assembles a homemade flying kit so that he and his young son, Icarus, can escape the tyranny of King Minos on the island of Crete; the air offers the only escape route because Minos rules the waves. The birdlike wings Daedalus constructs are held together by wax. Icarus gets off to a flying start, only to begin enjoying himself too much: he ventures too high, the wax melts in the sun, he gets into a flap, and the last we see of him is when he plunges into the sea. The bereft father is devastated, but in the second half of the Daedalus sequence, he shows a rather different side. He has a young nephew, Perdix, a precocious lad who's already cut his teeth as an inventor in his own right:

> The child was a boy
> of high intelligence, twelve years old, and responsive to
>     teaching.
> He'd even observed the pattern of bones on the spine of a fish
> and taken that as a model, cutting a series of teeth
> in a strip of metal and so devising the common handsaw.
>
> (8.242–46)

Jealous of Perdix, Daedalus tries to murder him by pushing him from a great height. Miraculously, Perdix is saved when Minerva turns him into a partridge in mid-fall; he gives his name to what he becomes, as the Latin for partridge is *perdix*. This transformation provides the "official" metamorphosis for the entire Daedalus-Icarus-Perdix storyline in book 8. Beyond this literal metamorphosis, however, various other modes of change are woven into this sequence: human becomes birdlike in taking to the skies; Daedalus changes from doting father to murderous uncle; and the Icarus story is itself transformed if, in retrospect after the Perdix episode, the tragedy of Icarus's demise is viewed as a payback of sorts for what Daedalus did to Perdix.

Here is yet another good example of how perspectives are constantly shifting, appearances deceive, and "reality" is always a work in progress in the *Metamorphoses*. But consider now a particular aspect of Daedalus's shifting characterization as he prepares for takeoff in the Icarus episode:

> Next he instructed his son: "Now, Icarus, listen carefully!
> Keep to the middle way. If you fly too low, the water
> will clog your wings; if you fly too high, they'll be scorched
>     by fire.
> Fly between sea and sun. No need to determine your course
> by Boötes, the Bear, or Orion's naked sword, like a sailor.
> Simply follow my lead."
>
> (8.203–8)

How old is Icarus? Earlier in the story we find him playing as Daedalus molds the wings:

> [he] smiled as he caught at the feathers fluttering in the
>     breeze;
> and now and again he would carelessly soften the yellow wax
> with his thumb, enjoying his game as he meddled and
>     interfered
> with his father's wonderful work.
>
> (8.197–200)

Is he five? Or perhaps seven at most? Whatever the case, we surely witness an adorable child still young enough to enjoy

Play-Doh. What matters is that Daedalus speaks to him in lines 203–8 in what sound like the clipped tones of the no-nonsense, white-coated engineer who uses words sparingly and with precision (think Q lecturing 007). The translation of lines 203–8 as just given captures something, but by no means all, of the syntactical density with which Daedalus delivers his instructions in Ovid's Latin: in lines 203–5, Daedalus's words in the Latin constitute a single sentence of six tightly woven clauses (labyrinthine in keeping with the mindset that designed the Cretan labyrinth?). And while he may try to keep things simple ("Fly between sea and sun"), the star names he lists in lines 206–7 add a touch of technicality that, we suspect, goes straight over Icarus's head. This loving father sheds tears of paternal tenderness, and he poignantly kisses his son just before they take to the skies. But that show of emotion can't entirely banish the thought that Daedalus hits the wrong note in his abrupt instructions to Icarus. His son needs gentle handling with kid gloves, but Daedalus appears more comfortable with the language of the user manual and out of touch with the childish excitement that inevitably causes Icarus to swoop and soar despite all killjoy orders to the contrary. In sum, Icarus's demise is in part a tragedy born of miscommunication and of Daedalus's insensitivity to his own weight of language: Icarus might have heeded him better if Daedalus had better heard the tenor of his own winged words and adjusted them accordingly.

## The Voice of Experience: Nestor Holds Court

Now for a much more controlled and controlling form of speech in the *Metamorphoses*. What's the real message, who is it aimed at (an entire audience, or just a select few within it, or even a single individual?), what's the true motive, and what's the intended outcome? How to assess the truth value of a given speech or anecdote or reminiscence, and how to guard against fakery? The *Metamorphoses* constantly tests our alertness to nuance and chicanery in the words spun by semiplausible or half-suspect characters—no bad training ground, perhaps, for how not to be taken in by truth twisters in our twenty-first-century echo chamber of sound bites, blog posts, tweets, exclusives, and infomercials.

Who better to illuminate us than the venerable Nestor, who had featured so prominently in Homer's *Iliad*—the legendary king of Pylos and the oldest and wisest of the Greek leaders at Troy? Nestor is already into his third century(!) when he appears in *Metamorphoses* 12. But despite his great age, he still commands a prodigious memory and still more remarkable energies as a raconteur who speaks nonstop for more than three hundred lines: long-lived, long-winded. He projects an air of easy improvisation at first, but he soon proves to be an adept performer when he embarks on his main showpiece: his eyewitness account (or so he claims) of a mind-boggling battle waged between the Lapiths and Centaurs at the wedding feast of Pirithoüs and Hippodamia. Pirithoüs was king of the Lapiths, a semilegendary race who lived in Thessaly in northern Greece, as did the Centaurs, creatures half-human and half-horse. This colorful cast of characters bodes well for the ripping yarn that follows. For all his wizened affability, Nestor knows all too well how not to let the truth get in the way of a good story, as we'll see in a moment; but first some contextualization.

Nestor's account of this battle between the Lapiths and Centaurs forms part of a sequence of episodes in *Metamorphoses*

12 and 13 that are related to the Trojan War. But even though this stretch of the poem is so obviously rooted in the *Iliad* in one way, it keeps its distance from Homer in another. Instead of focusing on events at Troy and on the familiar roll call of Homeric warriors on the battlefield, Ovid assembles an odd assortment of tangential episodes featuring relatively peripheral players (e.g., Cycnus, Caenis/Caeneus, and Periclymenus, all in book 12) who figure little, if at all, in the *Iliad*. Here is a decentralizing process, a sort of recasting of the Homeric script, that's taken a stage further when Ovid progresses to his mini-*Aeneid* that extends from late in book 13 to over half of book 14. Virgil's *Aeneid* was almost ten thousand lines long, but Ovid reduces its storyline to some one thousand lines of highly compressed retelling, conspicuous omission, and careful editing. What Virgil expands upon Ovid often contracts, and vice versa; Ovid applies to Virgil a technique that Virgil himself had already in some ways applied to Homer. An entertaining form of literary revisionism, certainly, but modifications of this sort amount to far more than just a literary game played for its own sake, to the effect that Ovid transforms the *Aeneid* into a form of "corrected" warm-up act for his own "authorized" version of events. No: the far more serious point is that by adjusting Virgil's choices of thematic emphasis, Ovid draws attention to the fact that the hallowed *Aeneid* is as much an exercise in editorial choice and manipulation as his own mini-*Aeneid* in books 13 and 14. The secret is out, as if it weren't already obvious to literary savants in the age of Augustus: the cultural authority of the *Aeneid* as a national epic of sorts is itself constructed, not heaven sent, and so always vulnerable to qualification, challenge, and

adjustment; and no less artificial and constructed, we infer, is the vision it propagates of Rome's evolution toward its culmination point in Augustus.

Against this background, Nestor's own careful editing when he tells his story—his eye for tactical omission, amplification, and controlled emphasis—illustrates from another angle this agile but fragile constructedness of meaning. His sleight of hand is already evident in his self-positioning in book 12 even before he launches into his blow-by-blow account of the Battle of the Bridal Breakfast. How does an aging warrior stay relevant when his best days are far behind him and a new generation of young bloods has superseded him? Nestor hasn't much to contribute in the way of battlefield exploits of his own when, during a truce in the Trojan War, Achilles and his entourage have a chance to relax a little and, over a glass of mulled wine, to mull over events on the frontline.

The talk turns to Achilles's victory over Cycnus, Neptune's son, whose divine lineage makes him impervious to injury. Achilles apparently assailed Cycnus with everything he had, but—to his increasing consternation—without drawing blood. He finally dashed him to the ground and throttled him, only for Cycnus to be transformed into a swan (hence *kuknos* in Greek) just when Achilles was about to strip his corpse: Achilles was thwarted once more. In the officers' mess Cycnus's immunity to injury is an object of wonder, only for Nestor at last to see his chance to regain the spotlight: he matches the Cycnus story by recalling that of a certain Caeneus, who was similarly invulnerable in battle. But, Nestor adds with apparent insouciance, Caeneus was also remarkable for another reason:

> His exploits won him renown, the more surprisingly so
> as he started life as a woman.
>
> (12.174–75)

Caeneus is briefly mentioned in the *Aeneid* (6.448–49): here is another example of Ovid playing up a story played down by Virgil. But what is Nestor really offering here? A throwaway line or a cunning lure? His audience is well and truly hooked, but none more so than Achilles—the only audience member, we suspect, Nestor is really trying to impress. Achilles takes the bait: "Out with the story, old Nestor! We're all of us eager to hear it" (177). Why is Achilles so curious to know the story? Caeneus's military exploits might certainly intrigue him, and perhaps he knows Nestor well enough to want to indulge the old man a little. But then a third possibility: Thetis, we recall, tried to disguise the young Achilles, her son, as a girl on the hideaway island of Skyros so that he wouldn't grow up to fight at Troy. Nestor knows exactly how to pique Achilles's interest: in remarking how Caeneus "started life as a woman," he touches with calculated indirectness on how Achilles too in a sense started life as a woman.

All eyes are now on Nestor, and even though he's far too old to wage battle, he proceeds to do the next best thing: he recounts the battle of all battles at the wedding reception of Pirithoüs and Hippodamia. But in keeping with the relaxed mood of the boozy soirée, he sensationalizes his über-epic by overlaying it with a Dali-like surrealism and touches of Pythonesque absurdity. Holding his audience is all, and he knows all the tricks of the trade. First, build up anticipation by delaying, delaying, delaying for as long as possible before you get to the point of your story—in this case, Caeneus's involvement in the battle. Second, maintain a quick tempo, keep changing your camera angles, have a rapid turnover of interesting characters, and always outdo yourself by reaching for ever more lurid and bizarre elaborations. Hence the increasingly outlandish forms of improvised weapon that start flying in a confetti of missiles: a huge antique wine bowl, an iron stand equipped with burning candles, the entirety of a smoking altar, the horns of a stag on which an eyeball gets stuck fast, the ripped-out shard of a mountainside, and so on (and on) as the violence gets lost in its own orgy of magical realism.

Third, pack your extravaganza with precise details about who did what to whom, when, and by what means, and add to the mix the quoted voices of the combatants to underscore that you really were there. An amazing feat of memory—but then forestall any potential doubters by invoking an unimpeachable witness to back up your claims. The hallowed seer Mopsus nicely fits the bill at the end of Nestor's anaconda of a thriller. Caeneus's ultimate fate in the battle is a little unclear, says Nestor: one report had it, he recalls, that he was crushed under the weight of a vast cluster of trees. But, said Mopsus (at least according to Nestor!), Caeneus was transformed into a bird that emerged from the woodpile. The seer's word was accepted by all ("The prophet said it and we believed it" [532]). Nestor is careful to close on this note of consensus, so that he can indirectly assert his own claim to Mopsus-like credibility, and he adds a solemn expression of grief for Caeneus for good measure before he closes: after hundreds of lines, or perhaps lies, of pure theater, Nestor knows all too well that to be truly (or falsely!) compelling, a sad story really must end in tears.

Nestor's sensational account surely appears far too good, or too fantastic, to be true. But how to call his bluff? How to draw the line between plausible fiction and impossible fantasy in Ovid's mythological wonderland? Thankfully in this case, help is at hand: beyond the transformation of Caeneus that is the official metamorphic centerpiece of the episode, Nestor's claim to credibility is itself seemingly transformed through the sudden intervention of Tlepolemus, Hercules's son. Hasn't Nestor omitted something important about the battle? Tlepolemus is miffed that his father hasn't been mentioned:

> "Sir Nestor," he cried, "I'm amazed that you have forgotten Hercules'
> glorious exploits. I'm sure that my father frequently told me
> the centaurs were conquered by *him*."
>
> (12.539–41)

Nestor elsewhere admits to the effects of aging, but he offers no such excuse here. In all honesty, it seems (but can we ever really trust him?), he attributes his deliberate omission of Hercules to his deep-seated hatred of him: Hercules had murdered Nestor's eleven brothers. Hence Nestor's self-justification:

> Now, Tlepolemus, handsome chief of the Rhodian fleet,
> do you really believe that I owe your father a public eulogy?
> Nevertheless, my silence about his exploits completes
> the vengeance I owe my brothers; my friendship with *you* is
> unbroken.
>
> (12.573–76)

So Nestor wrote Hercules out of his script because of a personal vendetta. Here is an egregious example of the truth being manipulated by a master of narrative control in the *Metamorphoses*, and Nestor may well have gotten away with it had a whistleblower not been on hand to expose his fraudulence. How much other fakery of this sort, we now wonder, may have passed undetected in so many other episodes thus far in the poem because there were no whistleblowers to call it out?

But then a further complication: in the mythological tradition, Hercules is more often associated with combat against the Centaurs in Arcadia, in connection with the fourth of his famous twelve labors (the capture of the boar of Mount Erymanthus), and not in Thessaly, the setting in book 12. Suppose Hercules was indeed involved in the battle that Nestor describes and that Nestor has airbrushed him out of the action: did Hercules really perform quite as heroically as Tlepolemus believes? Suspicion begins to fester, and two possibilities dawn. Did Hercules mislead Tlepolemus by exaggerating his exploits in the Thessalian battle? Or has Tlepolemus misinterpreted his father's account, confusing Hercules's achievements in Arcadia with his (lesser) exploits in Thessaly? Yes, Nestor faked it in cancelling Hercules from the proceedings in book 12, and Tlepolemus catches him red-handed. But how sure can we now be that Tlepolemus's own exposé is based on a true understanding of reliable facts? Or that he hasn't got the wrong end of the stick about Hercules's club?

> Thereafter, the episode abruptly ends:
> When the old man's story was finished, the wine went
>     round once again,

> and everyone rose from their couches to sleep for the rest
> of the night.
>
> (12.578–79)

After more than three hundred lines of high-octane special effects, how can Nestor's audience not be exhausted, whether through rapt fascination, sheer attrition, or not knowing quite what to make of the truth or otherwise of much or all of what they've heard? This long sequence in book 12 is hardly unique in the *Metamorphoses* in offering an object lesson in the control techniques of a skilled storyteller who knows how to manipulate an audience. But Nestor nevertheless stands out for his flexible approach to the truth, for his penchant for editing reality, and for his pure stamina: as he keeps going on, is the old man quietly baiting the Band of Brothers, as if testing the limits of their gullibility? He may be past it on the battlefield, but he's certainly no pushover in any battle of wits. And he's also a man of the future because he's no bad advertisement for how to be media savvy in the twenty-first century, how to deliver your truth, and how to mesmerize while adeptly improvising in a live-stream performance.

## The House of Rumor

The need to tread carefully as we try to decipher all the tones and turnings of Nestor's saga is already signaled early in book 12 by Ovid's treatment of *Fama*, or Rumor. This *Fama* has Virgilian DNA: in book 4 of the *Aeneid*, she is brought to life as a monstrous creation, horrible to behold, the superspreader of gossip about Aeneas's fateful liaison with the Carthaginian queen Dido. But Ovid departs from Virgil by focusing not so much on Rumor herself but on her dwelling place. His ostensible reason for visiting the House of Rumor just when he does in book 12 is to deliver the fast-breaking news: the Greek armada is on its way to Troy, and the Trojans have heard as much. His tour of the house may at first seem like an indulgent distraction at this pivotal dramatic moment, but let's dig deeper:

> Open by night and by day, constructed entirely of sounding
> brass, the whole place hums and echoes, repeating whatever
> it hears. Not one of the rooms is silent or quiet, but none
> is disturbed by shouting.
> . . . . . . . . . . . . . . . . . . . . . . . . . . . . . .
> The hall is filled by a crowd which is constantly coming
>     and going,
> a flimsy throng of a thousand rumours, true and fictitious,
> wandering far and wide in a turbulent tangle of language.
>
> (12.46–49, 53–55)

These lines gently evoke the noisy jostling of the Roman crowd and the hubbub of Roman political life—a touch of reality that nicely coincides with the quasi-historical turn that the *Metamorphoses* takes in books 12–15. The house is located in

> a space at the heart of the world, between the earth,
> the sea and the sky, on the frontiers of all three parts of the
>     universe.
>
> (12.39–40)

But the house is also significantly positioned in the poem from a symbolic perspective. It's central for two reasons: first, it sits on the borderline between the mythological meanderings down to the end of book II and Ovid's transition to the more historical stretches thereafter—a phase of the poem that follows a more orderly timeline in progressing from the Trojan War down to our final arrival point in Augustus's Rome. But second, and far more important: the House of Rumor is of central symbolic importance as an allegory for the swirl of voices that are heard throughout the *Metamorphoses*.

Consider the diversity of voices heard in this chapter alone—a mere fraction of all the whispers, claims, gossip, fabrications, pleadings, and evasions that crowd the fifteen books. The *Metamorphoses* is itself a vast echo chamber that teems with "a thousand rumors, true and fictitious, / wandering far and wide in a turbulent tangle of language" (54–55). That ultimate creator god of this world of voices, Ovid, imposes no regimented system of order on the free speech that runs riot in this polyphony: little or no fact checking, curbs on conduct, honor codes, or regulatory oversight to root out skullduggery or offensiveness and not much censorship or suppression except when the gods read mortals the riot act—a justice system that is itself deeply problematic, as we'll see in chapter 4.

The Creation out of chaos in book I was cacophonous, we recall, as the world-parts were brought to order, the skies thundered, and the winds raged. But a different chaos is unleashed when, after the Beginning, Ovid's mortals and gods find their voices. More or less at the poem's epicenter in book 8, just in advance of the Icarus story, Ovid introduces us to Daedalus by telling of his wondrous construction of the Cretan labyrinth as a prison for the half-human, half-bull Minotaur: Ovid's account of its bewildering network of bends, byways, and blind alleys (159–68) offers an irresistible metaphor for the treacherous textual labyrinth that is the *Metamorphoses*. But after the poem's mazy infrastructure is symbolized in the House of the Minotaur, the House of Rumor captures the vocal anarchy that rules the fifteen books: the erratic sound system conveyed in book 12 nicely complements the confusing floor plan emblematized in book 8.

Where to look for trust and stability within this vortex of voices and gridlock of competing agendas? We at last reach Ovid's climactic celebration of Augustus in book 15 after witnessing how so many characters struggle to control the implications of the words they use, how the Nestors of the world masterfully manipulate fact and fiction, and how the ripples of Rumor keep unsettling the textual flow: can anything remain reliable and certain in this treacherous flux? Our cumulative experience of the work conditions us to be wary, first to read Ovid's lines and then between them, and to take nothing, not even his praises of the emperor, for granted—no bad preparation, perhaps, for how to find direction through the mirror-maze of twenty-first-century image projection and social media. The word *fama* makes a final appearance in Ovid's prediction of his own lasting renown in the closing lines of book 15:

> Wherever the might of Rome extends in the lands she has
> conquered,
> the people shall read and recite my words. Throughout all
> ages,

> if poets have vision to prophesy truth, *I shall live in my*
> *fame.*

(15.877–79)

After all her slipperiness in book 12, *fama* is at last rendered fixed and firm, and Ovid breaks the golden rule of his *Metamorphoses* by eyeing changeless fame for himself. So what to make of an epilogue that runs counter to all that's preceded it? More of the same in its destabilizing irony? Or a volte-face that transforms everything? Nothing has changed, it seems, in this mixed message at the very end of our poem of change.

# 3

## The Path of Deviance

### Sexual Morality and the Incestuous Urge in the *Metamorphoses*

One of the most attractive features of the *Metamorphoses* is the rich diversity of the characters and personality types who populate Ovid's stories across the fifteen books. We sampled this diversity in the first chapter, but let's now consider his construction of character from a different standpoint. What, if any, are the standards and limits of "acceptable" conduct in this ever changeful Ovidian world, and who defines them? What code of morality, if any, can be inferred from the complex tapestry of human experience that takes shape across the poem? One immediate answer is that the gods hold mortals in check by punishing their transgressions; but the vagaries of divine justice in the *Metamorphoses* are for now another story, and one that warrants its own separate treatment in the next chapter. Our main concern here lies not with external systems of governance that police and punish mortal wrongs but with personal morality, and especially sexual morality.

The diversity of colorful characters in the *Metamorphoses* is matched by the endless variety of their often eccentric or outrageous behaviors, and many of those characters are at their most interesting when they're shown exploring their inner natures and proclivities. But what happens when that process of self-exploration strays into territory that is explicitly presented as morally challenging, controversial, concerning? True to the spirit of taking artistic liberties on so many fronts in the *Metamorphoses*, Ovid doesn't shy away from broaching this question through direct portrayals of extreme behavior. Take incest: he tells two notorious stories of incestuous desire, Byblis's passion for her brother Caunus in book 9 and Myrrha's union with her father Cinyras in book 10. In both cases Ovid presents incest as an unspeakable taboo, but what transpires is a remarkably detailed and searching examination of the impulses that drive Byblis and Myrrha to take the actions they do. The two episodes provide the provocation for what this chapter ultimately proposes: that after featuring these and other scenes of illicit or dubious desire, Ovid reins in such excesses in and after book 11, as if imposing a new discipline on his proceedings in advance of his climactic celebration of Augustus in book 15.

Ovid tells the Byblis story in book 9, but in book 10 he gives way to a secondary narrator: the legendary poet Orpheus, the mystical Elvis Presley of the Greek world who could charm all living things, and even rocks and trees, with his music (the Elvis analogy in fact extends back at least to Tennessee Williams's *Orpheus Descending* of 1957). Ovid's Orpheus proceeds to include the Myrrha story in the extended song cycle that he performs down to the end of book 10. We'll see that this transition from Ovid as narrator to Orpheus as subnarrator importantly conditions our understanding of the two incest stories. If, as we saw in chapter 1, Medea showed remarkable prowess as a poetic rival to Ovid, Orpheus poses a comparable challenge in book 10, albeit without the hard-edged aggression that Medea shows in book 7. When Orpheus dies at the start of book 11, we'll see that something dies with him: a poetic essence, an interest in sexual experimentation, a dynamic of "being different" and going against the grain. All this fades away with Orpheus's passing, as if a certain mode of eccentricity is curbed just at the moment when Ovid begins to redirect his poem to more conventional, Rome-centered ground: he moves in books 12–14 to the Trojan War and his mini-*Aeneid* en route to his praises of the House of Augustus in book 15. There's undoubtedly plenty of quirkiness still to come in the remarkable characters and strange scenarios we encounter after Orpheus's demise. But Orpheus still exerts a peculiar freedom of vision and maneuver that's lost when he departs from the *Metamorphoses*.

Orpheus runs freely, then, until Ovid writes him out of the poem—a tension between license and control that suggestively matches, in a different dimension, the efforts of both Byblis and Myrrha to curb the incestuous desires that consume them. One of the most affecting aspects of both episodes is the anguish with which Byblis and Myrrha articulate the conflict stirred by their yearnings. Here is a form of inner struggle that finds many resonances in a twenty-first-century context where young lives are so often encouraged to express an authentic, core self—an appeal to release our individuality, but one that's frequently hampered by social expectation and accepted norms, by the orthodoxies imposed via social media, or by the pressures of conformity to an idealized body type, say, or a fashionable look. In this respect, Byblis and Myrrha reflect in their incestuous urges a form of explored subjectivity and truth-to-self that—despite the troubling nature of their urges—commands a certain admiration as much for its courage as its raw honesty.

As for Ovid's Orpheus, he has just lost his beloved wife, Eurydice, in tragic circumstances. What happens to a mind that struggles to come to terms with an existence that's been turned upside down? We'll see that his experience of trauma has left him disoriented, self-absorbed, and trapped in an endless cycle of revisitation: he can't escape the reverberations of his personal disaster that keep infiltrating his song cycle. In our own times, and especially after the isolating effects of the COVID-19 pandemic, we've recently witnessed an increasing awareness in public discourse about matters of mental health, care of the self, and strategies of therapeutic intervention. No attempt will be made here to analyze Ovid's Orpheus from any forced and superficially applied psychotherapeutic perspective. But in our age of heightened sensitivity to mental well-being, Orpheus's song cycle repays close attention as a sympathetic and delicately drawn portrait of a mind in private turmoil.

To return to Byblis and Myrrha, they react very differently to their inner struggles: despite the obvious similarities between their storylines, the two episodes are far apart in their deeper meanings. At the most basic level, whereas Byblis is thwarted in her incestuous designs, Myrrha manages to consummate her longed-for union with her father; and whereas Byblis is slow to recognize what's problematic about her incestuous stirrings, Myrrha's sense of guilt is acutely felt right from the outset of her story. But the most telling divergence between them lies in their differing abilities to hold their incestuous impulses in check. In many ways, both stories are concerned more with the control of sexual yearning than with the satisfaction of it, and the shock effect of the tales disguises the finer psychological probing that goes on within them. Let's take a closer look at the two cases, then, in the process of developing our larger argument: after the incest narratives and the racy Orpheus song cycle of books 9 and 10, the *Metamorphoses* undergoes a form of thematic "correction" as it moves into its last five books. Its moral climate has to be recalibrated, even sanitized, in readiness for Ovid's endpoint in Augustus in book 15.

## The Story of Byblis, Brook, and Caunus

Ovid may at first appear sternly judgmental when he introduces Byblis's story in book 9 ("Byblis' fate is a warning against prohibited love" [454]), but his tone proves to be far more compassionate than condemnatory as the tale takes its course. The storyline: despite her initial efforts to persuade herself that her feelings for her brother Caunus are natural enough, Byblis gradually recognizes her "forbidden desire" (502) for what it really is. Unable to contain her secret any longer, she reveals all in a letter to Caunus that's delivered by a trusted servant. Disgusted by the revelation, Caunus rounds on this messenger with an almost murderous fury; let's not forget this nasty little encounter, as it will matter later. But Byblis won't give up. She keeps trying to woo Caunus, and when he flees the country in desperation, she goes after him with a crazed but futile obsessiveness. Exhausted by her efforts, the endlessly weeping Byblis eventually melts away into a spring that flows with her own tears. In a first internal monologue, Byblis conceives her letter. We then witness her in writing mode as she composes the fateful missive. Finally, after the letter is rejected by Caunus, in a second monologue we hear Byblis's bitter regret at having sent it. Three speech acts on Byblis's part, then, all of them painfully revealing about her innermost feelings: she's an open book, as her name already implies through its punning play on the Greek βύβλος/βίβλος (*bublos/biblos*, "papyrus," hence "book").

Ovid's is the sole extant version of the Byblis myth that explicitly features her penning a letter to Caunus. Elsewhere in the tradition, she appears to approach her twin not in writing but with a spoken confession of her love for him. Short of imagining that her letter is a casual Ovidian innovation of no great consequence, what are we to make of this fresh turning as Byblis puts her stylus to wax?

Let's consider the matter from two angles, first by viewing Byblis's letter in relation to Ovid's earlier experimentation with poetic epistles. In his *Heroides*, we remember from chapter 1, famous women in the annals of Greco-Roman myth (Penelope, Medea, Dido, etc.) write letters to the male lovers who've in various ways abandoned, deceived, or mistreated them. Byblis's missive is cast in a different meter—dactylic hexameters, not the elegiac couplet. But more important is that she departs from the model of female authorship in the *Heroides* by writing in a different key and with a different tactical intent. The *Heroides* are full of the anguish of separation, anger at infidelity and betrayal, hope for reconciliation, and resignation to loss. They almost invariably presuppose a preexisting relationship, but Byblis's letter is proactive, not reactive: she writes in order to launch a relationship, not to rescue, renew, or rue one.

Byblis's missive has rather more in common with the function of letter writing in Ovid's *Art of Love*. There, in book 1, the male lover is urged to make initial contact with the object of his affections via a letter that uses all the tricks of the trade: lots of flattery, entreaties, sweet persuasion, "words that play the lover" (1.439–40), any number of promises—the goal is to break the ice, then very possibly a heart. Equivalent advice is given to the women addressed in book 3 of the *Art of Love*—advice on how to receive, interpret, and reply to the letters sent by their admirers; on the plain style appropriate for such replies; and on the need for disguise and secret communication so that no suspicions are aroused. Above all, the letters of both the male and female schemers have to be coy and careful. They must never reveal the author's full hand or even the author's real scribal hand; and they must use duplicity as a means either of seduction or of denying responsibility if a compromising document ever comes to light.

How well does Byblis do by the exacting standard Ovid sets for letter writing in the *Art of Love*? She makes no attempt to disguise her authorship by having another pen the letter to her dictation. She tries to hide her identity, but it slips out soon enough:

> Your lover wishes you well; and unless you respond to her greeting,
> she'll never be well in herself. She's ashamed, so ashamed to give you
> her name; but if you would know my desire, I wish I could argue
> my cause without disclosing my name till my prayers are answered,
> my hopes are fulfilled, and you acknowledge and call me—your Byblis.

(9.530–34)

In the body of the letter she bares her soul; she's achingly sincere and direct where Ovid as Professor of Love would urge obliqueness and dissimulation. Before handing this most intimate of documents to one of her servants, she "nervously flattered him, saying: 'My friend, I know I can trust you'" (569): has she really conducted a proper background check as Ovid's pupil in the *Art of Love* surely would? But there's a more general problem: as a first approach to the object of her desires, hers is a "male" letter in terms of the instruction offered to Rome's Lotharios-in-training in *Art of Love* I. There, Ovid's apprentices quickly learn to use letters as weapons of mass seduction. But Byblis seems to lack fluency in that cynical code, as if embarking on a masculine form that goes against her gender and her nature. It's oddly fitting that the wax tablets fall from her hands when she gives them to her favored attendant for special delivery—an ill omen that anticipates Caunus's enraged response when he reads only part of the letter before hurling it down. Byblis has been much too hasty, as she herself acknowledges in her second internal monologue: her cardinal mistake was to write the letter in the first place and to resort immediately to the fixity of the written word instead of testing Caunus's openness to such an approach by "sound[ing] his feelings out beforehand, by carefully / dropping mysterious hints" (588–89).

The second angle on her letter that concerns us for now lies precisely in Byblis's over-hasty transparency: she writes with the same flood of feeling that characterizes her manner in her two internal monologues. In the first of those monologues she reflects on her "dream in the night" (474)—her dream of union with Caunus:

So long as I never attempt to commit such a sin in the
    daytime,
it doesn't matter how often it happens at night in my dreams.

(9.479–80)

But as Byblis's monologue progresses and she gradually sub-
verts her own efforts at resisting her incestuous urges, the dream
at night gives way to what increasingly looks like a follow-on
reverie by day. And that continuity of dream experience is
matched by the same habits of thought that carry over from her
monologue to her letter. Take her mannerism of autocorrection
and revision in her monologue:

But what's in a dream?

Can it have any substance?—Yet even a dream can come
    true, perhaps.
May the gods forbid it!—But gods have certainly slept
    with their sisters.
Saturn was married to Ops, whose blood was the same as
    his own;
Ocean and Tethys are husband and wife, like Juno and Jove.
But the gods have rules of their own. It is idle to measure
    our human
codes and customs against the different conventions of
    heaven.

(9.495–501)

With each "yet" and "but" here Byblis keeps qualifying herself—a stop-start approach that she carries over to her writing
as she begins her letter and then hesitates, "writ[ing] on the

wax, then curs[ing] what she'd written; / inscribing and then deleting, emending, rejecting, approving; / alternately putting the tablets down and picking them up" (523–25). Yet despite these staccato corrections, the overall flow of her words in her two monologues—more than forty lines in both cases—is as copious as her open-heart effusions in her full tablet, "so full indeed that the final line was scrawled in the margin" (565); and that copious flow is then matched by her ceaseless tears after she's changed into a spring.

It's perhaps time to rename Byblis so that we can try to capture in English these many interrelated facets of her character, just as Ovid does in playing on Byblis's name and the Greek *bublos/biblos*. Let's try calling her Brook: Brook she is when we first meet her, B(r)ook when we find her to be an open book as we read her letter, and brook she becomes when she dissolves into her own tears at the story's end. Brook is like the brook because both are transparent and exhibit a sort of permanent fluidity: just as the spring is continuous in one way, ever changeful in another, so in speech and script Byblis flows and checks herself through revision or erasure and then keeps on flowing. Brook is like a book because she's easy to read in the transparency of her feelings, and within Ovid's text there is literally no difference between her spoken and written words: we read her interior monologues just as we read what she writes to Caunus, so that Brook is in a sense always a book.

Where is Caunus in all this? He speaks only once in the entire episode, in outraged reaction to Byblis's letter:

> Young Caunus was simply appalled and had only read part
> of the message

before he suddenly flushed with anger and threw the thing
   down.
Then scarcely refraining from striking the terrified
   servant's face,
he shouted, "Get out while you can, you vile incestuous
   pander!
You'd pay with your life, if your murder wouldn't disgrace
   my name."
The poor wretch took to his heels and reported this savage
   reply
to his mistress.

(9.574–80)

Caunus is shocked into gale-force fury. But what precisely
motivates quite this pitch of anger? He presumably reads only a
few lines of Byblis's letter when he suddenly comes to a grind-
ing halt at the sight of her name. If he recognizes Byblis's hand
and thinks that she's truly penned the letter (as opposed to its
being a clever forgery), he instantly perceives the wretched go-
between as Byblis's abettor; *he* receives the blast that Caunus
might otherwise have directed at his sister. Reputation evidently matters to Caunus. Why otherwise say that the servant
would pay with his life "if your murder wouldn't disgrace my
name"? Caunus takes flight when Byblis persists in wooing him
even after her letter has been disastrously received: his reputation is again at stake, and he avoids all possible danger or rumor
of any incestuous association with her by getting away as fast as
he can.

Caunus appears staunchly upright so far, but let's now probe
a bit further. Does he react to the attendant as he does because

the letter touches a raw nerve? Various versions of the Byblis story circulated in Ovid's time. According to one of them, it was Caunus who fell in love with his sister; when he couldn't shake off that yearning, he fled far from home to avoid acting on his desires. Ovid was adept at exploiting competing strands of a given myth in developing his storylines in the *Metamorphoses* and elsewhere, often with breathtaking effects in terms of dramatic irony. Against this background, does Caunus have something to hide in *Metamorphoses* 9?

The whole episode is transformed when we see a new possibility: Caunus has an incestuous desire of his own for Byblis, but he's too ashamed and too concerned with reputation to act on that impulse. He may also suppose that Byblis would recoil in horror if he made an advance in her direction; for he has no inkling, we imagine, about her own incestuous stirrings, at least until the fateful letter arrives. Why does he recoil when he suddenly discovers that she shares his guilty passion? His concern for his good name again gets in the way. But does he also suspect that the buried truth about him has somehow leaked and that the go-between who delivers the letter knows all too well that Caunus has a dark and potentially compromising secret? Hence his murderous outburst, and hence he throws down the letter: he wants nothing to do with the matter, and least of all to make himself vulnerable to the pleadings of a lengthy and perhaps dangerously enticing letter. When he runs away from home to avoid Byblis's continuing advances, he's also running away from himself. He flees, we suspect, because he also senses how Byblis now plans to approach him, and he makes sure to avoid it: the softly-softly approach to wooing him that Byblis contemplates in her second internal monologue has a far better chance of winning him over than did the bolt from the blue delivered by her letter.

The upshot of these suspicions is that a fresh perspective transforms this moving story—let's call it a metamorphic shift of viewpoint like that which changes our take on Daedalus in the Icarus and Perdix sequence in book 8 (as we saw in chapter 2). What may at first appear to be the one-sided story of Byblis's incestuous yearning turns out possibly to be a double story, with Caunus no less inclined in that direction than his like-minded twin. But their responses to their urges couldn't be more different: the painful transparency with which Byblis reveals her inner anguish is diametrically opposed to Caunus's suppression of his deep-seated desires, and the result is an agonizing battle of incestuous wills. She's out of control, he's all about control; she's an open book, he's a closed one; and the episode is ultimately concerned as much with burying desire as it is with Byblis's irrepressible need to release it.

## Underground Music: Orpheus's Song Cycle

After Byblis's frustrated yearnings in book 9, Ovid moves to a new extreme in book 10 when the incestuous deed is done and the seed sown: Myrrha is impregnated by her father, Cinyras. This episode, the main feature of book 10, may well have been importantly influenced by a now-lost miniature Latin epic on the same topic by the first-century BCE poet Gaius Helvius Cinna. But the poet who concerns us most for now is Orpheus: early in book 10 Ovid hands the microphone to his charismatic subnarrator, and it's Orpheus who tells the series of stories that occupies the rest of the book. It's important to view the Myrrha episode in the context of his full song cycle: in trumping Byblis, Myrrha acts with a degree of carnal license that's in keeping with the risqué edginess, even the flat-out bizarreness, of Orpheus's larger storytelling.

Fittingly for our poem of change, this Orpheus is himself a figure transformed from the Orpheus who stars in the obvious model for the start of book 10: Virgil's treatment of the story of Orpheus and his wife, Eurydice, in the fourth and last book of his *Georgics*. That work is ostensibly a didactic poem on agriculture, but it's also vitally engaged with (among much else) humankind's relation to the natural world and the rhythms and dictates of the cosmic order. In the *Georgics*, Orpheus's story is one of tragic loss through his own impulsiveness—a momentary lapse that undoes all the hard work by which Orpheus almost succeeds in bringing Eurydice back from the dead after she accidently steps on a snake and is killed by its venomous bite. Heartbroken, Orpheus descends to the Underworld to try to retrieve her. Charmed by his music, the infernal powers allow Eurydice to return to the living, but on one condition: that Orpheus lead his wife to the surface without once turning back to look upon her during their ascent. Alas! They've almost reached the upper world when, in a moment of madness, Orpheus can't help but glance back at Eurydice; the damage done, he's lost her for a second time, and for good. For seven months thereafter he lies beside the River Strymon in Thrace, entrancing the beasts and trees with his sad song of lament. "No thought of love or wedding-song could bend his soul" (*Georgics* 4.516): spurned by Orpheus's ongoing devotion to Eurydice, "the Ciconian women [of southern Thrace] . . . tore the youth apart amidst their divine rites and midnight Bacchic revels, and scattered him over the wide fields" (520–22). Yet as his severed head was swept along by the River Hebrus, still his voice "called with fleeting breath on Eurydice—ah, poor Eurydice!" (525–26).

After the dignified solemnity with which Virgil captures the tragedy of Orpheus's double loss, we're in for a shock when we encounter Ovid's version of the Backward Look at the start of *Metamorphoses* 10: it's impish in its flippancy, as if deliberately puncturing the delicate sentimentality of Virgil's rendition. Take the song with which Orpheus charms the Underworld and wins permission to lead Eurydice back upstairs. Virgil leaves it to his reader to imagine how Orpheus pitched that all-or-nothing performance. But Ovid delivers it verbatim, casting Orpheus as an obsequious supplicant whose rhetoric appears more grimly functional and made to measure than sublimely inspired as a tearjerker of a cri de coeur. Then we find all the hardest-core criminals in the Alcatraz of the Underworld suddenly spellbound by Orpheus's music and distracted from their usual tortures. We're tastelessly shown Eurydice limping as she follows her husband to the upper world, trailing along as best she can on her wounded foot. And in Virgil she utters five lines of unbelieving anguish and tormented farewell after Orpheus's disastrous glance backward; but in Ovid she manages only a one-word "goodbye" (*vale* [62]).

Amusing effects, or perhaps bemusing ones, and there are many more of them in this opening sequence in book 10. But what's important for now is that they set the tone for the strangeness of feel and content that pervades the entire book, and that the stories Orpheus goes on to tell belong within a very particular timeframe in Virgil. All Virgil says is that, as Orpheus lay by the River Strymon strumming on his gently weeping guitar, he "unfolded his tale [i.e., the story of his loss of Eurydice], charming tigers and drawing oaks with his song" (*Georgics* 4.509–10). Ovid expands on this Virgilian discography: we're to imagine that all the songs recorded in *Metamorphoses* 10 were included in Orpheus's repertoire by the Strymon in *Georgics* 4.

This distortion of Virgil is only the first in a sequence of peculiar developments in *Metamorphoses* 10, of quirky psychological and physical/sexual scenarios, and of an increasingly eccentric tendency in Orpheus himself. Consider his track record: he's very nearly achieved the impossible by going to the Underworld and raising the dead, thereby overturning the cosmic order, only to be thwarted at the last moment by his mad rush of impulse. It's as if this sum of experience has messed up the ordinary coordinates of his existence and made any reversion to a "normal" life impossible. And now that nature's laws have been overthrown, his own nature undergoes its own convulsion of change. No thought of love or wedding song could bend the soul of Virgil's Orpheus, as we've seen. But in *Metamorphoses* 10 there's a more extreme development:

> Orpheus now would have nothing to do
> with the love of women, perhaps because of his fortune
> in love,
> or he may have plighted his troth for ever. But scores of
> women
> were burning to sleep with the bard and suffered the pain
> of rejection.

Orpheus even started the practice among the Thracian
tribes of turning for love to immature males and of
    plucking
the flower of a boy's brief spring before he has come to his
    manhood.

                                                (10.79–85)

Against this background of seismic upheaval, disorientation, and personal loss, *of course* the stories that Orpheus goes on to tell are going to be unconventional, a bit weird, even salacious and kinky, and full of highly charged emotions.

Orpheus gives a foretaste of this walk on the wild side when he announces that he'll start his song with Jupiter, but not with an epic rendition of Jove's famous victory over the rebellious Giants in the battle of all battles, the so-called Gigantomachy. It was a familiar trope among Roman poets in the lighter genres such as love elegy to make a great show of rejecting heavyweight martial epic for the featherweight poetics of the slender Muse. Orpheus buys into this technique by turning his back on old-school, Gigantic epic. But instead of settling for the heterosexual love poetry that we associate with the Roman elegists such as Propertius and Ovid, he pushes the envelope by announcing a racier topic:

Now there is call for a lighter note. Let my song be of boys
whom the gods have loved and of girls who have been
    inspired to a frenzy
of lawless passion and paid the price for their lustful desires.

                                                (10.152–54)

True to his pledge that he'll start with Jupiter, Orpheus begins by telling the story of how Jove, in the form of an eagle, raped the Trojan youth Ganymede. Orpheus then progresses to the tragic story of Hyacinthus, Apollo's young darling: he's killed by a discus that was hurled by the god and rebounded off the ground, smashing the beautiful boy in the face. It was an accident, but Apollo is wracked with guilt nonetheless, and he movingly promises a permanent memorial for Hyacinthus in the form of the hyacinth flower that grows from the boy's blood. After the cosmos is created in *Metamorphoses* 1, we recall from chapter 2, the first god we witness is Jupiter in ruthless action: he avenges Lycaön's wickedness by inflicting a catastrophic flood on the entire human race. The next god prominently featured in book 1 is Apollo, Daphne's witless but terrifying pursuer. When Orpheus starts his song in book 10, his movement from Jupiter to Apollo offers a miniature replay of Ovid's running order of the gods in the macroscheme of the *Metamorphoses*. But there's a playful if sinister twist. Instead of the tyrannical Jupiter, we find Jove in love. Jupiter's passion (or lust) has been stirred on numerous occasions in the *Metamorphoses* already, and the list of his rape victims is long; but here for the first time in the entire poem he reveals an appetite for *male* rape.

Orpheus's depiction of Apollo is a bit more uplifting. In contrast to the clownishly insensitive Apollo who traumatizes Daphne in book 1, the Apollo who mourns Hyacinthus in book 10 is a god transformed. He's a far more sympathetic figure who's now apparently capable of introspection and true remorse as he grapples with his own feelings of responsibility for the accidental death. But this remaking of Apollo is also revealing about Orpheus. Let's listen carefully as Apollo bemoans Hyacinthus's unlucky fate:

> I see your wound, and I see my guilt.
> You are my sorrow and you are my shame. You died by my
>     hand,
> and so shall your epitaph say. I, I am the cause of your
>     death.
> Yet how can it be my fault, unless to have played a game
> or have fondly loved can be called a fault? How I wish I
>     could die
> in your place or beside you! But since we are subject to
>     destiny's laws,
> you can only survive in my heart, be recalled in the words
>     of my lips.
>
> (10.197–203)

It's surely hard to separate Apollo's ruminations here from Orpheus's own experience of losing Eurydice. "I, I am the cause of your death" (199): in having Apollo take responsibility for the boy's death, does Orpheus indirectly address his own feelings of guilt for his fateful backward glance? Yet—to reapply Apollo's words—how can it be Orpheus's fault, unless to have fondly loved Eurydice can be called a fault? How he wishes he could die in her place or beside her! Orpheus almost managed to bring Eurydice back from the dead, only to be bound by destiny's laws when he loses her for a second time: does he look for a crumb of comfort in the thought that even Apollo, the god of medicine, was powerless to defy those laws in Hyacinthus's case? No wonder Apollo is sympathetically drawn in this episode: Orpheus's turmoil as he struggles to come to terms with his loss of Eurydice reverberates in the mixture of guilt, shame, self-exculpation, and resignation that he attributes to Apollo.

This reflexive turn in Orpheus's storytelling is a recurrent feature of his entire song cycle, and it poignantly captures his inability to move forward or to recenter his existence after Eurydice's return to the dead. You get the sense that the deeply personal resonances of his cycle reflect a residual form of PTSD born of post-Eurydice shellshock and that the lingering effects of this trauma are recreated in flashback memory moments across the cycle. Let's quickly sample three aspects of this reflexive phenomenon before we explore how the Myrrha episode fits into the broader pattern of such introspection.

First, various of Orpheus's stories highlight the disastrous consequences of unthinking impulsiveness. Even before he settles into his song cycle, the story of Cyparissus is neatly forward looking in this respect. Among the "arboreal throng" (106) that forms Orpheus's audience is the cypress tree. Cyparissus, Apollo's darling, had a beautiful pet stag that was accidentally killed "when a sharp spear pierced him, unthinkingly thrown" by the boy (130). Grief-stricken, Cyparissus begs Apollo to let his tears fall forever, and he's turned into the cypress, that familiar Greco-Roman symbol of mourning. As if taking his cue from Cyparissus's story, Orpheus soon embarks on the tale of another of Apollo's darlings, Hyacinthus. Cyparissus was unthinking, *imprudens* (130), in hurling the spear that killed the stag. Hyacinthus is similarly *imprudens* (182) in dashing after the discus that tragically kills him when it rebounds off the ground and smashes into his face. Later in the cycle, Adonis, the mortal lover of Venus, ignores her advice to

> avoid all kinds
> of creatures that won't turn tail but bare their teeth for a
>     fight.
> Avoid them, I beg you. Don't let your courage destroy us
>     both!

> (10.705–7)

Adonis doesn't listen ("Warnings, however, are never heeded by courage" [709]): he impulsively chases after a boar, and he's fatally wounded when the beast turns on him and buries its tusks deep in his groin. Then the story of the swift-footed Atalanta, whose suitors must beat her in a footrace if they're to win her hand in marriage: one suitor in particular, Hippomenes, may seem impulsive in trying his luck against the odds ("Fortune favors the brave!" [586]), but his prospects are transformed when Venus grants his prayer for help. She gives him three golden apples, and he uses them to distract Atalanta during the race. When Hippomenes strategically drops the apples one by one along the way, it's her impulsive desire to go after them that enables him to win both the race and the apple of his eye. Impulsiveness was Orpheus's undoing when he glanced back at Eurydice: by harping on the theme of unthinking rashness in his song cycle, he keeps revisiting that central facet of his own tragedy.

Second, there's the matter of divine justice: Orpheus features various human excesses that are duly punished by the gods, especially Venus. After the Hyacinthus episode, Orpheus seems to go out of his way to stress just deserts, not random chance, by replacing the tragedy of the innocent boy's accidental death with the punishments that befall willful sinners. On Venus's Cyprus, a murderous race of Cypriots pollutes the altar of the guest god, Jupiter Hospes, with the sacrificial blood of human guests. Outraged, Venus transforms them into horned bullocks (called the Cerastae, literally "horn wearing" in Greek)—suitable victims for sacrifice themselves! They get their comeuppance, as do the daughters of Propoetus in Orpheus's next breath: they deny Venus's divinity, only for the goddess to retaliate by transforming them into prostitutes; hardened by that experience, they're subsequently turned to stone. Later in the song cycle Hippomenes and Atalanta feel her wrath. Despite Venus's help with the golden apples, Hippomenes failed to offer thanks after winning Atalanta. Venus reacts by arousing a great passion in Hippomenes to make love to his new wife, and he does so in a shrine of the goddess Cybele. As punishment for profaning the shrine, Cybele changes them into lions. In all these cases Venus takes action in response to a flagrant human provocation. Does Orpheus gently invoke them to underscore his own relative blamelessness in losing Eurydice? Or might he imagine that he too has been persecuted by the goddess of love? If so, he quietly stresses through the contrasting cases of the Cerastae, etc., that he for one is hardly a committed and flagrant offender who gets what he well deserves.

Third, miracles sometimes happen when the gods are moved to grant mortal prayers, as we saw in the case of Hippomenes and the golden apples he receives from Venus. But a still more spectacular miracle occurs in Orpheus's famous story of the sculptor Pygmalion—a tale that's significantly placed just before the Myrrha episode. The daughters of Propoetus are turned by Venus first into prostitutes, as we've seen, and then to granite. Scandalized by their vice-ridden ways, Pygmalion carves "an amazingly skilful / statue in ivory, white as snow, an image of perfect / feminine beauty—and fell in love with his own creation" (247–49). When Venus's festival comes round, Pygmalion prays to the goddess to be allowed to wed "a woman resembling my ivory maiden" (276). Intuiting his deeper meaning, Venus grants Pygmalion's prayer, his statue is brought to life (contrast Propoetus's daughters being turned to stone!), and the two are happily united as husband and wife.

There's a lot going on in this outlandish and titillating story, as we might expect from an Orpheus whose lived experience has blurred the boundary between life and death, the upper world and the lower, sexual normativity and otherness. Pygmalion shows a distinctly creepy side as he fondles and kisses his nameless statue, dresses her in finery, and "girdle[s] the breasts with elegant bands" (265): it's a real turnoff to see just how turned on he is by every touch and fondle, each nudge and whisper, as if a repressed male who's indulging his own fantasy. In shaping this idealization of what he wants womanhood to be, he's hardly interested in anything beyond her purely physical form. Nothing is said of his creation's inner essence and her qualities of character or personality after she's brought to life; it's as if all he wishes for in praying to marry her is her guaranteed virginal purity. In this respect, his initial misogyny ("he chose for a number of years / to remain unmarried," 245–46) doesn't disappear when his dream woman comes to life; if anything, the special sculpting of his custom-designed lover confirms his loathing of womankind more generally.

Orpheus too, we recall, shunned women after he lost Eurydice: she is to him what Pygmalion's statue is to the sculptor—irreplaceable, the love of his life, the only woman who ever really mattered. But Pygmalion comes out well ahead in a direct comparison of his and Orpheus's fortunes. A woman is brought (back) to life with divine help in both cases; but whereas Orpheus loses Eurydice through his own folly just when he's on the verge of final deliverance, Pygmalion's prayers are fully answered in his happy ending of a story. Can we avoid interpreting the Pygmalion tale as a displacement exercise by which Orpheus tries to console himself with a storyline that works by analogy, channeling his own narrative of loss toward a different, far happier outcome? But then, of course, there's the ultimate futility of the exercise: Orpheus's loss is arguably only aggravated by the impossibly escapist dream that he indulges through Pygmalion. Yet that dream also fails to account for the psychological possibility that Giulio Bargellini captures so well in his 1896 *Pigmalione* in figure 3: when the sculpture comes to life and extends her charms to her maker, the shock of her seductiveness causes Pygmalion to recoil in what looks like a mixture of astonishment, horror, and self-protection. His fantasy can sustain itself, it seems, only as long as he controls it; as soon as she begins to control the situation as in Bargellini's rendering, stone no more, he looks petrified.

At last to the Myrrha episode itself. But in many ways we've already anticipated a key feature of this episode by considering Orpheus's reflexive turn in the scenes that surround it: shouldn't we by now expect the Myrrha story to be at least partly tinged by aspects of his own experience and subtextual psychodrama? Cinyras, Myrrha's father, was Pygmalion's grandson: given

Figure 3. Giulio Bargellini, *Pigmalione*, 1896.

*Source*: Galleria Nazionale d'Arte Moderna e Contemporanea, Rome.
Photo copyright Scala / Art Resource, NY.

their shared descent from Pygmalion, it's no great surprise that
both Myrrha and Cinyras are sexually unconventional—she in
lusting incestuously after him, he with a thing for girls of his
daughter's age. Whereas in book 9 Byblis takes time to recognize the deviance of her yearnings for Caunus, Myrrha knows
right from the start of her story that her passion is guilt-edged.
She battles hard against it and even prepares to commit suicide
to escape her sinfulness. But her nurse saves her from hanging
herself and then draws the terrible truth out of her. The nurse
subsequently becomes Myrrha's enabler, seeing to it that the
drunk Cinyras takes Myrrha into his bed. He thinks he's having sex with someone else, a girl of Myrrha's age, and his
daughter is careful to leave his darkened chamber before the

daylight exposes her real identity. Their assignations continue for several nights until Cinyras is curious to know who the girl is. Her terrible truth comes to light, Cinyras rages, and the now-pregnant Myrrha runs for her life. She roams far and wide until she collapses out of exhaustion and shame. Not wanting to live yet hating to pollute the dead by passing away, she prays to the gods to "refuse me life and refuse me death by changing my form" (487). Her prayer is answered when she's transformed into a myrrh tree that endlessly weeps tears of resin.

What to make of this story at this point in Orpheus's song cycle? Coming as it does after the Pygmalion episode (where Pygmalion-qua-creator in a sense "fathers" the woman he later marries), Myrrha's story takes to a new, incestuous extreme the expansive sexual geography that's already been mapped out in the cycle. Beyond this escalation of apparent perversity, however, Orpheus's censorious tone at the start of his tale ushers in a mimetic effect that becomes more pronounced as the episode progresses—his odd mirroring of Myrrha. "It's a shocking story," he says:

> Keep far away from here, daughters,
> far away, fathers. Or, if you cannot resist my poems,
> at least you mustn't believe this story or take it for fact.
> If you do believe it, then also believe that the crime was
>     punished.
>
> (10.300–3)

What's Orpheus really saying here? For one thing, he's in the middle of nowhere, singing before an audience of beasts, rocks, and trees. He's dreaming if he thinks his warning to fathers and daughters to close their ears serves any real purpose whatsoever—unless, that is, his performance is truly a dreamlike projection here, as if he magically transports himself from the Thracian wilderness to a purely fictive theater of the imagination. Shut your ears! But this prohibition is also an indirect encouragement to listen hard ("if you cannot resist my poems" [301]); and after saying you mustn't believe the story, he all but encourages belief in it ("If you do believe it" [303]). He wants to have it both ways, it seems, condemning a lewd story while simultaneously keeping us interested and egging us on. This technique of squeezing the brake while wanting to press the accelerator closely resembles Myrrha's condition within the storyline: fully aware of her guilty passion from the outset, she tries to hold it in while part of her desperately wants to let it out. Hence she prays to the gods to "avert this terrible evil; resist the crime in my heart" (323), only then to backslide when she continues with: "if this is indeed a crime" (324). It isn't a crime for animals to mate incestuously: why, she argues, should it be so for humans? Yet she soon reverts again ("But why am I talking like *this*? / Such thoughts are forbidden, I must dispel them!" [335–36]).

Myrrha's tragedy lies to a large extent in the agonizing prolongation (for a hundred or so lines!) of this stalemate between passion and constraint, stop and go, until she aims to settle matters once and for all by preparing to commit suicide. Whatever license animals have to commit incest, she can't shake off her obedience to the ordered way of things at the human, societal level:

> No, Myrrha, so far your body
> is free from the taint of sin. Do not sin in your mind; you
>    must not
> defile great Nature's unbreakable bonds with incestuous
>    union.

(10.351–53)

In his different way, Orpheus too of course knows a thing or two about disrupting the natural order of things; and when we look more closely, certain suggestive overlaps between his own experience and Myrrha's soon come into view. Let's begin by revisiting his appeal to fathers and daughters to steer well clear as he embarks on his story: the Latin wording here, *procul hinc, natae, procul este, parentes!* (300), explicitly echoes the words of Virgil's Sibyl in the *Aeneid* as she and Aeneas are about to enter the Underworld to visit his father Anchises's shade: *procul, o procul este, profani* (6.258: "Away, away, o you that are uninitiated!"). The echo is deeply ironic: in contrast to Aeneas's act of filial piety in visiting Anchises in the Underworld, Myrrha's will be a deceitful, truly impious interaction with *her* father. As she enters Cinyras's chamber and she's guided onto the bed by the nurse (that grotesque caricature of Virgil's Sibyl), it's pitch black in the dead of night: Myrrha descends into a symbolic Underworld, and Ovid's Orpheus takes quite a liberty by travestying Virgil's hallowed scene in this way.

But are we right to think only of Aeneas's visit to the Underworld? What about Orpheus's descent? After all, consider the situational similarities between his plight and Myrrha's: she's only too aware of her guilty passion and tries hard to suppress it before finally succumbing to it and entering the Hades-like bedchamber. After losing Eurydice for the first time and making his way down to the Underworld, Orpheus tells the assembled infernal powers that

> I'd hoped to be able to bear my loss and confess that I
>    tried.
> But Love was too strong.
>
> (10.25–26)

Like Myrrha, Orpheus tried to suppress an urge that became overwhelming. He had to make at least the attempt to retrieve Eurydice, but

> [i]f fate forbids you to show my wife any mercy, I'll never
> return from Hades myself. You may joy in the deaths
>    of us both.
>
> (10.38–39)

Orpheus craves death if he can't win Eurydice back. For her part, Myrrha too sees death as the only option if her passion for Cinyras must remain unfulfilled: she has many suitors, but Cinyras is the only man she lusts for. After Orpheus loses Eurydice for the second time, "scores of women / were burning to sleep with the bard" (81–82), but he's not interested: Eurydice is the only one, matchless and irreplaceable. Then there's the license granted to both Myrrha and Orpheus to get what they want. After succeeding in his appeal to the Underworld gods, Orpheus "was told he could lead [Eurydice] away" (50). Seeing that Myrrha is set on dying if she can't indulge her passion, her nurse takes charge of the situation by announcing that Myrrha *will* obtain her father (Latin *potiere* in line 429, literally "take possession of"). After Cinyras discovers the truth and Myrrha flees, Myrrha prays to be allowed neither to live nor to die, as we saw earlier—an in-between condition that's suggestively paralleled by Orpheus's ambiguous mixture of being half-alive and semidead. He's a living misfit in the Underworld but like a lifeless shade when he returns to the upper world without Eurydice.

But then yet another surprise. Cinyras is at last eager to know his lover's identity (*avidus cognoscere amantem* in the Latin [472]). Now compare Orpheus as he makes his ascent with Eurydice "and, eager to see her, he longingly turns his eyes to her" (*avidusque videndi / flexit amans oculos* in the Latin [56–57]): in his unfortunate eagerness to see, he's just like Cinyras. Orpheus's storytelling here is beginning to take on an incestuous feel of its own in his symbolic association first with the daughter, then with her father. The gender fluidity resulting from this identification with both the female and male protagonists adds yet another dimension to the pattern of transgression that's fundamental to the entire episode. Both Myrrha and Orpheus descend into the darkness and disrupt the natural order in doing so: Orpheus has in effect largely retold his own story through a sexualized reimagining of it, and the lurid sensationalism of the incest is ultimately of far less interest, perhaps, than the mindset that leads him to steer, complicate, and queer the story in all the ways he does.

## The Straightened Path to Augustus's Rome

Orpheus's song cycle expires at the end of book 10, but his life story spills over into the beginning of book 11: the effect is to compartmentalize the cycle within its own special space, as if a sequestered part of the poem where his transgressive imagination is allowed to run freely. After Orpheus is killed and his body is torn apart by the Ciconian women in the opening lines of book 11, his shade eventually passes under the earth and goes looking for Eurydice:

> As he searched the Elysian Fields,
> he found the wife he had lost and held her close in his
>    arms.
> At last the lovers could stroll together, side by side—
> or she went ahead and he followed; then Orpheus ventured
>    in front
> and knew he could now look back on his own Eurydice
>    safely.
>
> (11.62–66)

Orpheus is dead happy to be reunited with Eurydice and to be able to look back upon her without peril. A pleasing picture, but through that reunion, his turn toward pederasty in book 10 is also reversed—part of a process by which the sexual otherness of the song cycle, the self-referential inflections of his storylines, and the eccentricity of his overall manner are finally reined in, finished, contained. A distinctly otherworldly chapter of the *Metamorphoses* comes to an end when we finally say farewell to Orpheus.

Many more stories of a bizarre kind are recounted as Ovid accelerates into the last five books, and many of the tales he tells retain a strong erotic charge. At the end of book 11, for example, Aesacus, an illegitimate son of King Priam of Troy, pursues the nymph Hesperia: he inadvertently causes her death when a snake bites her in the foot as she runs away from him, and he struggles to live with his guilt after her passing—a sequence of events that strongly evokes the story of Orpheus and Eurydice, at least until Aesacus is changed into a diver bird who continually tries to do away with himself by plunging headlong into the waves. In book 12, Caenis is raped by Neptune and then transformed by the god into a male, Caeneus, so that she can never again be subject to female violation. In book 13, the Cyclops Polyphemus only has eyes, or his one eye, for the nymph Galatea. As she lies in the arms of her beau, Acis, she overhears Polyphemus practicing the "Love, love me do" with which he means to woo her; but when he sees Galatea with Acis and realizes the futility of his romantic ambitions, he reverts to monstrous form by killing Acis. Circe, Picus, Pomona: the amorous stirrings, strivings, and sufferings of all these figures and more, some of them famous but fleeting in the poem, others obscure but lingering, fill out the love interest of books 11–15 in all sorts of colorful ways. But despite the persistence of this erotic component far into the poem's final third, there's clearly a shift of thematic emphasis after Orpheus has left the building early in book 11.

There's no incest in the last five books, no explicit or extended focus on pederasty, no Pygmalion-like grooming, no prostitution, no profaning of shrines through steamy shenanigans on the altar. Yes, there are rapes and hostile pursuits, and from a twenty-first-century perspective all such violence constitutes a deeply disturbing feature of Ovid's poetics. There are several graphic descriptions of shocking physical suffering earlier in the poem, but that appetite for grisly detail is far less apparent in the final third; and even in the battle of the Lapiths and Centaurs in book 12, Ovid describes the mind-boggling violence in terms that are far more cartoonish than truly chilling in their sensationalist overload (see chapter 2). Some stories of unrequited love end badly, as in the case of Iphis in book 15—a male Iphis who's not to be confused with his namesake in book 9, the one who featured in chapter 1. Spurned by the beautiful but cold-hearted Anaxarete, this Iphis commits suicide; shocked by the death she's precipitated, Anaxarete is suitably frozen into a frigid statue. But there's a notable proliferation of more harmonious relationships late in the poem: Ceÿx and Alcyone in book 11; the sweetheart Centaur pairing of Cyllarus and Hylonome in book 12; Acis and Galatea in book 13; Aeneas and Lavinia, Vertumnus and Pomona, and Romulus and Hersilië in book 14; and Numa and Egeria in book 15. Some of these couplings are Happy Ever Afters, some scarred by tragedy, but all contribute to the casebook of heterosexual and marital conventionality that predominates as the poem moves toward its climax in Augustus himself—Augustus and Livia, that is, his "blessed wife" (15.836). We've already touched (in the introduction) on the legislation introduced by Augustus to promote marriage and procreation and to curb adultery. By reverting to this more normative vision of romance in the final books, does Ovid move with the times? In advance of his imperial praises at the end of book 15, we infer, he's gradually adapted his poetics to suit the moral climate of Augustus's Rome.

The quirky Pythagoras who stars in book 15 is perhaps Orpheus's closest kindred spirit in the *Metamorphoses*. Remember how in chapter 2 the Pythagorean theory of the soul's transmigration was seen radically to challenge Ovid's commitment to metamorphosis as a one-time, permanent change? What if, instead, the soul is constantly and open-endedly recycled from one bodily existence to the next? But Pythagoras wasn't believed—or so we're told just before Pythagoras starts talking; Ovid thereby moves to neutralize the Pythagorean theory even before it's launched. Pythagoras is only the latest in a sequence of characters who pose a threat to Ovid's authorial control in the *Metamorphoses*. After Medea's brazen attempt to hijack the poem in book 7 (as we saw in chapter 1), Orpheus presents a different challenge in book 10: if the *Metamorphoses* has at times already strayed into areas of perverse psychosexual behavior through the likes of Narcissus, say, or Byblis, that streak of deviance is taken yet further in Orpheus's song cycle. After his death at the start of book 11, the exotic foibles of the flesh in book 10 are behind us, the final third appears much more restrained in sexual matters, and we find ourselves on the reassuring road to Augustus's Rome in book 15. Nor should we forget (in chapter 1) Bacchus's presence as a quiet infiltrator of minds and *mores* after he enters the poem in book 3. Medea, Orpheus, Pythagoras, Bacchus: all pose significant challenges to Ovid's mission in the *Metamorphoses*, which is to bring the poem "down to my own lifetime" (1.4), but it's Mission Accomplished when he finally hails Julius Caesar and Augustus in book 15. Augustus succeeds where Medea et al. have failed, it seems, in that he alone is able to dictate the course of Ovid's entire poem and to draw it relentlessly, inexorably, inevitably to its august conclusion; he alone is an insurmountable force field of attraction.

But Ovid's soaring epilogue ("Throughout all ages . . . I shall live in my fame" [15.878–79]) vies with, and may even trump, that crowning celebration of Augustus. And how long is it before we develop a certain nostalgia for the waywardness of an Orpheus or for the eccentricity of a Pythagoras? In hindsight, wasn't life in the *Metamorphoses* so much more colorful, more interesting, before the Augustan force of gravity applied its weight of obedience at the end of book 15? There's perhaps cause for lament, then, and not just for Orpheus's death: the lights go out when his shade finally descends to the Stygian darkness early in book 11, and extinguished with him is the quirky but arresting flame of brilliance that was his song cycle in book 10.

# 4

## Rough Justice

### Victimization, Revenge, and Divine Punishment in the *Metamorphoses*

Let's pick up where we left off at the end of the last chapter and take a closer look at Ovid's triumphant epilogue to the *Metamorphoses*:

> Now I have finished my work, which nothing can ever
>      destroy—
> not Jupiter's wrath, nor fire or sword, nor devouring
>      time.
> That day which has power over nothing except this body
>      of mine
> may come when it will and end the uncertain span of my
>      life.
> But the finer part of myself shall sweep me into
>      eternity,
> higher than all the stars. My name shall be never
>      forgotten.
> Wherever the might of Rome extends in the lands she has
>      conquered,
> the people shall read and recite my words. Throughout all
>      ages,

if poets have vision to prophesy truth, I shall live in my
fame.

(15.871–79)

By "Jupiter's wrath," *Iovis ira* in the Latin, Ovid means light-
ning here: as if a physical monument made of unbreakable
material, his *Metamorphoses* is immune to destruction through
any natural force. But given Augustus's assimilation to Jupiter in
his own lifetime, it's impossible not to recognize the emperor in
this allusion to the god. As soon as we tune into this Augustan
wavelength, Ovid's envoi to the poem becomes edgy and competitive, Augustus deified but defied. Ovid's temporal arc in the
poem ran, we recall (from the introduction), "from the world's
beginning / down to my own lifetime" (1.3–4). The epilogue at
the end of book 15 is now clarifying: the poem culminates not in
"my *Augustan* times" but in "*my* times"—*Ovid's* Now, a Now
extending into the limitless expanse of his postmortal fame.

The *Metamorphoses* was more or less complete when, in 8
CE, Ovid's life was suddenly turned upside down by Augustus's banishment of him to Tomis, on the western coast of the
Black Sea. In the wake of his exile, the epilogue of the *Metamorphoses* instantly reads differently. Ovid's spirited cry that his
work is invulnerable to Jupiter's wrath now projects either a
brash and rash confidence before his downfall or a steely resilience after it. In Tomis, Ovid wrote two collections of plaintive
elegiac missives; the first was entitled *Tristia* (*Poems of Sadness*),
the second *Epistulae ex Ponto* (*Letters from Pontus*). In the first
book of the *Tristia*, probably composed in 8–9 CE, Ovid reverts
once more to the language of Jupiter's wrath, *ira Iovis* in the
Latin (1.5.78), but this time very much as the chastened victim

of Jupiter-Augustus. Later in the book he articulates his personal metamorphosis in terms of the *imago* or portrait of him that the *Metamorphoses* now represents. He is transformed, and so too is his poem of change by the new six-line preface that Ovid envisages for it at the end of *Tristia* 1.7:

> "All you who touch these rolls bereft of their father,
> to them at least let a place be granted in your city [Rome]!
> And your indulgence will be all the greater because these
>     were not published
> by their master, but were rescued from what might be
>     called his funeral.
> And so whatever defect this rough poem may have
> I would have corrected, had it been permitted me."
>
> (1.7.35–40; trans. A. L. Wheeler)

These lines are written in the elegiac meter, not the epic hexametrical form that Ovid had used in the *Metamorphoses*. If we imagine the six lines as a new opening to his poem of change, that work is visually and metrically metamorphosed by this elegiac preface. But it's also radically recast by showing us a poet who's now diffident and deprived, his magnum opus as if almost destroyed along with Ovid on his figurative funeral pyre.

Legend had it that Virgil's dying wish in 19 BCE was for his unfinished *Aeneid* to be burned after his death. Ovid appropriates that legend for himself in *Tristia* 1.7 in claiming to have tried to consign his own incomplete *Metamorphoses* to the flames when he was exiled; so much for his crowing confidence in the epilogue to book 15 that nothing, "not Jupiter's wrath, nor fire or sword," will destroy his work. But what matters most for now is the power shift that this imagined elegiac preface to the *Metamorphoses* represents. The butterfly that was the preexilic Ovid has been crushed by the Augustan steamroller, and his lament that he'd have revised the faults in his *Metamorphoses* "had it been permitted me" is as chilling as it's poignant. For all Ovid's fame and flame of brilliance, Augustus's cold hand of authority wields inscrutable power: his decisions are clinical, non-negotiable, final.

This chapter is all about the inscrutability of power, and not just in the *Metamorphoses*: the exilic end of things will play an important role when, later in the chapter, we consider Ovid's own fate in the light of that suffered by many of the poem's characters. Ovid *requires* us to approach the *Metamorphoses* with this eye on Augustus. Already in book 1, in the Lycaön episode that we touched on earlier (see chapter 2), the assembly of the gods that Jupiter convenes gathers in "the mighty Thunderer's / royal palace," a place "I'd not be afraid to describe as the Palatine Hill of the firmament" (170–71, 176): it's as if the Roman senate and emperor are in session. Later in the same passage, Ovid gushes that

> just as your people's loyal devotion is welcome to you,
> Augustus, so was his subjects' to Jove.
>
> (1.204–5)

This explicit linkage of god and emperor so early in the arc of the poem conditions us to view Jupiter through an Augustan lens for the entirety of the fifteen books—and perhaps to read the many instances we encounter of Jupiter's high-handedness as prompts to reflect on the harsher or more impenetrable aspects of Augustus's rule.

## Heaven Knows: The Willful Gods of the *Metamorphoses*

It's a commonplace that the gods of the *Metamorphoses* are all too human in their flaws and often more flawed even than humans: small-minded, peevish, cruel, manipulative, and deceitful, they demand respect from mortals without always (or ever?) deserving it. Anger is a defining characteristic of several of the leading Olympians, but Ovid was of course hardly the first Greco-Roman poet to rile up the gods in this way. So in Virgil's *Aeneid*, for example, Juno's anger in many respects drives the action, hostile as she is to Aeneas because of her longstanding hatred of Troy. But Virgil's epic explores the nature and the intensity of that plot-defining hostility right from the outset and questions it with an almost philosophical sense of mission ("Can there be such great anger in the minds of gods?" [1.11]); and Juno's anger is ultimately brought to a dignified resolution when she and her husband, Jupiter, are reconciled late in the epic. A good measure of the difference between Virgil's sober and somber epic vision and Ovid's lighter, more sprightly touch lies precisely in their divergent treatments of divine anger. In the *Metamorphoses*, the gods' anger is often petty in its causes, unprincipled in its actions, vicious in its consequences for others, and impervious to the kind of reasoned resolution that wins over Juno in Virgil. Jupiter's first appearance in the *Metamorphoses* is ominously colored with anger ("Mightily angry, as only Jove can be angry" [1.166]), but he's also prolific in rousing Juno to anger. Her wrath is a persistent feature of the poem, but it differs from the long-term, obsessive hatred that characterizes her in Virgil; in Ovid, she's more prone to sharp flashes of anger, especially in connection with Jupiter's infidelities.

But what about those on the receiving end? Angry outbursts on the part of gods whose actions are erratic, exploitative, and devoid of any moral compass leave lesser beings dangerously exposed in the *Metamorphoses*. How do we make sense of a world in which the gods are free to act as they will, with few if any curbs on their behavior? A world in which they often treat mortals, especially women, as mere commodities to be abused and discarded? The *Metamorphoses* is notorious for its many episodes of sexual exploitation and rape, graphic violence, and macabre cruelty. Much of this violence is perpetrated by the gods. Over and above the excruciating details of such scenes, it's disturbing to observe that after the multiple rapes committed by the gods in the early books, the first instance of human raping human occurs only in book 6, where Tereus brutalizes Philomela (more on this ghastly scene in a moment). Already before then, the range of offenders has begun to widen out, as in the case of the river god Alpheüs's pursuit of Arethusa in book 5; and it soon expands further to include the likes of the elements (the North Wind, Boreas, Orithyia his victim late in book 6), the Centaur Nessus early in book 9 (he unwisely tries to despoil Hercules's wife, Deïanira), and the mortal hero Peleus in book 11 (his attempted rape of Thetis; this before she succumbs to him in a separate encounter). The example set by the gods in the early books spreads like a contagion among these other constituencies as the poem advances. And the steady accumulation of these attacks across the books has a numbing effect of its own, as if normalizing such practices in the cruel world of the *Metamorphoses*.

It is no surprise that the *Metamorphoses* has caused considerable unease in its twenty-first-century readership because of the sexual aggression and exploitation that are graphically portrayed when Daphne, say, is pursued and traumatized by Apollo in book 1 or when Pygmalion craves the woman he carves from ivory in book 10. These disturbing features of the *Metamorphoses* have to be frontally addressed if it's to hold its place in the modern classroom or public library: they can't just be excused or explained away by appeal to the male-dominated sociocultural context in which Ovid was writing. Certainly, Roman society was traditionally patriarchal and highly militarized, and sexual violence was encoded in Roman self-identity through the foundational legend of the rape of the Sabine women under Romulus in the eighth century BCE (the abduction was meant to expand Rome's protopopulation). True, things had changed considerably by the end of the Roman Republic in the 30s BCE, especially for upper-class women. The practice of *manus* (literally "hand"), whereby a woman's control of property and even her right to life were ceded to her husband, had long ceased to be commonplace. Holding their own property, women could build considerable fortunes of their own. They could divorce, many were educated, and even though very few female writings survive to attest directly to their enhanced status and increasing independence, they are often portrayed as strong individuals; and while their societal role as mothers and wives remained primary, that role was sanctified as a great strength for the common good. Yet despite these positive developments, episodes of violence against women were common in Roman theater and pantomime in Ovid's time. Highly sexualized murals adorned the walls of the rich. Roman slaves were especially vulnerable to abuse because they didn't own their own bodies. In Roman law, the definition of rape, criminal liability for it, and the severity of punishment for it depended in large part on the victim's status. In these ways and more the *Metamorphoses* reflects the broader cultural climate in which it was composed. But the sheer scale of Ovid's appetite for graphic portrayals of physical and psychological trauma in general, and of sexual violence in particular, nevertheless remains as undeniable as it is unnerving, even abhorrent, in a twenty-first-century context.

This chapter makes no attempt to play down these features of the *Metamorphoses*. It focuses instead on another side of the picture, and from two angles. First, power exercised without transparency or consistent process; second, open protest and retaliation against that intransigent power. To begin with the first angle: episode after episode presents us with autocratic dictators-of-action, humans as well as gods, who do as they will, often with shocking outcomes for the victims of their deceit, resentment, violence, or neglect. Injustices abound, and that's the point: justice itself is something lost, craved, complicated, or called for in what amounts to a litany of license across the books. Here the shadow of Augustus looms large once more: in a fictional world where injustice has so many permutations and justice is a moving target, how can we not begin to question, through Ovid's promptings, how justice functions under the first Roman emperor, in many ways that law unto himself?

Then the second angle of approach, on protest and retaliation: for all the horrors inflicted on humans, especially women, in the *Metamorphoses*, there are conspicuous cases in which victims at last call out their persecutors and rise up against them, often by taking justice into their own hands. Certainly, protected as they are by their immortality, the gods are largely immune to any lasting consequences of this fighting spirit. And these pockets of resistance are also more the exception than the norm in the lawless free-for-all that dominates large swathes of the poem. But in this modern age of the #MeToo movement, a moment when the masters of the universe have at last been exposed and denounced by the voices they long suppressed; in this age of increased action against sex trafficking, on-campus sexual assault, and harassment and discrimination in the workplace; in this time of a new reckoning with historical injustices such as racial inequality, wealth disparities, and barriers to social advancement, the *Metamorphoses* is in important ways empowering even despite its accent on violence. Again, this is not to underestimate the extent and degree of the cruelty that the poem inflicts on innocent victims, especially women. But in turning the spotlight on the abuses perpetrated by the inscrutable powers that be and by unleashing voices to speak up and out against their oppressors, the poem has important protest value—*it speaks a message of urgent modern relevance*—even before Ovid signs off by defying Jupiter's wrath at the end of book 15.

Silence itself is capable of speaking volumes in the *Metamorphoses*, sometimes as a prelude to unspeakable cruelty—an ominous retreat from words that's taken to a sadistic extreme in the Tereus and Philomela episode of book 6. There, the vile Tereus first speaks in his reported voice in Ovid's text only some one hundred lines into the story, when he's at last managed to entrap Philomela so that he can indulge the lust for her that he's long stored up ("Tereus cried out, 'I have won! My prayers are answered, she's sailing / beside me!'" [6.513–14]). Tereus's lack of words before this point offers but one example, albeit a truly shocking one, of silence as a dangerous internalization of cruel urges in the *Metamorphoses*. But silence is also frequently imposed as a form of coercion and punishment in the poem, and so it proves later in the Philomela episode. Let's begin with her story, and then work outward from there in exploring the anatomy of justice in the *Metamorphoses*, but with our focus on empowerment, not subjection: on breaking the silence, speaking truth to the featureless face of authority, and daring to defy the forces of oppression.

## The Female Fight-Back Begins

A quick glance back at book 3 usefully sets up our introduction to Philomela and her sister, Procne, in book 6. The first murder perpetrated by a mortal woman in the *Metamorphoses* comes late in book 3, in a story we've already touched on briefly in chapter 1: Agave, a devotee of the god Bacchus and infatuated by his intoxicating influence, murders her own son Pentheus, king of Thebes. As if hallucinating in her Bacchic trance, Agave, along with her fellow Bacchantes (the familiar term for the god's devotees), mistakes Pentheus for a boar and ruthlessly hunts him down, dismembers him, and decapitates him—a harrowing episode that's complicated by Agave's diminished responsibility for her actions. The second act of female killing is Procne's murder of her young son, Itys, in book 6. It's important to see this second outrage in relation to Agave's crazed killing of Pentheus: whereas Agave is off her head when she takes Pentheus's head off, Procne murders her son with ice-cold calculation; and whereas Agave is a truly frenzied Bacchante, Procne feigns Bacchic infatuation at a critical moment in the sickening story of her sister Philomela's rape and mutilation.

The plotline in book 6 goes like this. Philomela is sadistically raped by Procne's husband, the savage Tereus, king of Thrace. To silence Philomela, he cuts out her tongue, which—in a moment of shocking tastelessness—is shown twitching on the ground, wriggling "like the quivering tail of an adder that's chopped in half" (559). Silenced and imprisoned, Philomela weaves a tapestry that is surreptitiously delivered to her sister, thereby revealing the crime to Procne. Here is Procne's feigned Bacchante moment: during the annual festival of Bacchus, the disguised Procne rescues Philomela in a frenzy not of Bacchic infatuation but of sheer rage. Then for her carefully orchestrated revenge against Tereus: she steels herself to kill and cook her son and subsequently serves him up on Tereus's dinner plate. Tereus begins to gorge himself, he asks for Itys to be summoned, and Procne gleefully reveals to him the terrible truth: Itys is already there! Tereus can't stomach it; he's instantly maddened with fury and anguish, but with no flicker of remorse for what he did to Philomela. In his rage he goes after Procne and Philomela, and during the furious chase that follows all three are changed into birds.

This story is importantly positioned both within book 6 and in the larger flow of the *Metamorphoses*. The first four stories of book 6 down to line 400 all center on the divine punishments incurred by human presumption and, in one case, by the satyr Marsyas's ill-advised challenging of Apollo to a piping contest; these stories raise difficult questions about the harshness of the penalty in relation to the severity of the offense, as we'll see in due course. Philomela is the third female victim in book 6, but the gods now recede from what plays out here as a purely human drama. The turning point of the story, and indeed of book 6, comes when Philomela gets word out to Procne via her tapestry. This silent message shocks Procne into a state of grief-stricken silence of her own, but one that's also ominous as she quietly plots her revenge:

> Amazing to tell, she said not a word.
> All speech was choked by her grief. The words that she
>      needed weren't there
> to express her outrage. Tears were forgone, as she rushed to
>      confound
> all right and all wrong. Her heart was totally set on revenge.
>
> (6.583–86)

Whatever ambiguities complicate our weighing of justice in the first four stories, here for the first time in book 6 the mortal victim fights back—Philomela through Procne, a secondary victim in her own right—and the violator is punished. We've yet to address the troubling implications of Procne's murder of Itys, but our focus for now is on Philomela finding her voice after Tereus has ripped out her tongue: the ingenuity she shows not only powers her revenge but also reverses the pattern of female victimization and exploitation that has predominated so far in the poem.

Let's briefly consider two illustrations of this victimizing tendency, the first of them supplied by Io late in book 1, in the next episode after the Daphne sequence. Like father, like son, or vice versa in Ovid's ordering of his stories: after Apollo's harrowing pursuit of Daphne, Jupiter sees the beautiful Io and tries to seduce her, but when she starts to run away he cuts off her escape route and rapes her. Juno is suspicious: where on earth is Jupiter? The comic air of Jupiter's exchanges with Juno as he tries to hide what he's up to with Io only serves to intensify the helplessness of Io's plight. A major challenge for Ovid's modern readers (it's far harder to gauge how his readers reacted in his own day) is that he tells Io's story with a jaunty levity in places and even a disturbing glibness. The many incidents of rape in the *Metamorphoses* are recounted in different registers, some more graphic and explicitly violent than others, but few (the Daphne episode in book 1 perhaps a case in point) with anything that looks like a truly affecting pathos and engaged empathy for the victim. So here: Jupiter disguises Io as a cow, only for the suspicious Juno to demand the cow as a present; Juno promptly puts the beauteous bovine under the watchful eye (in fact, the hundred eyes) of the monster Argus. Jupiter is not done yet: he sends Mercury as a hit-god to murder Argus, only for Juno to vent her fury at her sentinel's death by "sending a horrible demon to frighten the eyes of Io / by day, and her mind at night" (725–26). The harshness of Io's plight is merely underscored by the flippancy with which her agony is finally eased: after a couple of lines of quick appeasement from Jupiter, Juno is placated, Io is restored to human form, and "she nervously tried a few words in her long-lost language" (746). As a cow she could only emit "a hideous lowing" (637), and it's painful to observe her frustrated efforts to communicate with her father, Inachus, and her sisters. All she can do is sketch out two letters "traced by a hoof in the dust, / which revealed her name and the sorry tale of her transformation" (649–50): a neat play on *Iō* and the Greek exclamation of grief, *iō* ("alas!")

Io manages to express herself, yes, but with no immediate change for the better: when her father manages to decode the hoofmarks, he reacts with resignation and despair. Even Io's retransformation into a nymph brings only a happyish ending to her story first of rape and then of Juno's pique and persecution— happyish because she's "saved" only by a quirk of divine whimsy (but then better news: she ultimately ends up worshipped as the goddess Isis). And even though Juno relents for now, her vicious streak soon resurfaces in our second illustration of a victim's voicelessness, the story of Callisto in the middle of book 2. Jupiter chose his words very carefully when he swore to Juno that Io "will never provide you with cause for vexation / again" (1.736– 37). Io may be out of the picture, but what about other targets? The Arcadian virgin Callisto, a devotee of Diana, catches his eye. He deceives her in the guise of Diana, but "his subsequent felony gave him away" (2.433). She fights back against her rapist but uselessly so. When her pregnancy comes to light, the real Diana casts her from her circle, and, after giving birth to a boy called Arcas, Callisto is persecuted by the resentful Juno. Transformed into a bear by Juno, she loses her powers of speech, instead emitting only menacing growls and anguished groans. To complete her torment, she is scared of wolves, even though her own father, the Lycaön we encountered in chapter 2, is one of them.

Raped by Jupiter, then tortured by Juno, Io suffers terribly, but Callisto's treatment is even worse: Diana and Juno make her pay for Jupiter's initial outrage, and as a bear she comes close to being killed by her son Arcas's javelin. Jupiter saves the day by transforming both mother and son into neighboring constellations, Ursa Major and Ursa Minor—only for Juno's fury to be ignited once more. Io and Callisto aren't the only characters who are harshly punished and imprisoned by speechlessness in these early books of the *Metamorphoses*, but book 6 at last brings a new development via Philomela's tapestry: here *for the first time in the work* a mortal overcomes her speechless state to spark the fight-back against her oppressor—a shift from the passive to the active voice, so to speak, that marks a turning point for human female empowerment in the poem. And the trend continues: it's surely no accident that we witness the formidable Medea (albeit a mortal with divine ancestry via her grandfather, Helios) very soon after, right at the beginning of book 7.

## Divine Vices, Mortals Left to Their Own Devices

But what about Procne's shocking murder of Itys, her darling boy, so that she can feed him to Tereus? Procne functions as a sort of alter ego for her sister, as if all the barbaric violence that's been inflicted on Philomela now explodes outwardly through Procne's savagery. Hence the horrific vision of Philomela's tongue twitching on the ground is matched by all the graphic details of Itys being killed and cooked by Procne and then consumed by Tereus. This isn't just sensationalist, chamber-of-horrors writing for its own sake but a pitch of grotesquerie that resets the coordinates of female capability in the poem: in a world of vicious cruelty where the gods are more often persecutors than saviors (witness Io and Callisto!) and the likes of

Tereus act with inhuman abandon, Procne fights fire with fire, albeit with troubling consequences for how we view Itys's death in particular. We weep for the boy, and the eyes of Procne herself well up with tears before she steels herself for her hard sacrifice; yet the ultimate responsibility for Itys's murder arguably lies with Tereus, not Procne. We're getting into deep moral waters here, pleading mitigating circumstances in one heinous case so as to see punishment duly done in another. Even as Ovid shows the sisters triumphant, he's radically problematized the nature of justice in this Wild West stretch of the poem.

However we decide the rights and wrongs of this case, the shifting perspectives it provokes contribute to the metamorphic complexity of the episode. In causing us to contemplate a given scene or action from different or developing viewpoints, Ovid here and elsewhere (the Daedalus episode in book 8, say, or the Byblis episode in book 9, as we saw in chapters 2 and 3, respectively) renders the very act of reading a metamorphic experience: a first impression meets the eye, only then to be transformed by a new twist in the plotline or qualified by a fresh consideration, such as how we process the shock of Itys's murder. But the sisters' actions remain troubling for yet further reasons. Punishing a human monster like Tereus is one thing, but vengeance against gods who commit atrocities is quite another: for all the empowering implications of the Philomela-Procne episode, the likes of Io and Callisto model a form of victimization by the gods that persists well after book 6. Then there's the poignant sight of humans trying to do the right thing, living blameless lives and showing pious devotion to the gods in an Ovidian world where the gods themselves aren't too troubled by moral scruple. In exploring this distance between gods and mortals, Ovid takes up a major preoccupation in the Greco-Roman poetic tradition from Homer and Hesiod onward; but the Roman times in which he's writing also influence his portrayal of human morality.

Take the matter of the marital stability that Augustus's moral legislation aimed to promote. Several notable couplings are landmarks of devotion in marriage despite the ups and downs of the many tangled relationships that are strewn across the *Metamorphoses*. We can perhaps see in these unions a glimpse of the Augustan ideal—a form of relief from all the sexual shenanigans that begin with Jupiter himself. Juno constantly has to keep a close eye on his roving eye, a tendency of his that should give us pause: we need to be careful about when to remind ourselves of Augustus's assimilation to Jupiter.

Let's quickly sample some of these happy unions. In book 1, only a few mortals survive the flood that Jupiter inflicts on the entirety of the human race; this as follow-up to his punishment of the impious Lycaön. Two of the survivors are Deucalion and Pyrrha: these models of mutual devotion and god-fearing simplicity are duly rewarded when they are shown (via a riddling oracle of Themis, the goddess of justice) how to set about repopulating the earth. In book 8, the elderly Philemon and Baucis entertain two strangers—Jupiter and Mercury in human disguise—with humble but heartwarming hospitality. Their generosity is set in stark contrast to the hostility that the gods encounter among Philemon and Baucis's neighbors. The gods punish those neighbors by inflicting a flood on them, but they exempt Baucis and Philemon from the general punishment (a rerun of sorts of Deucalion and Pyrrha's survival of the earlier flood); the story ends with Jupiter granting them any wish they desire, whereupon they promptly ask to be appointed as the guardians of his temple that their cottage has become. They are paragons of devotion to each other as well as to the gods and also to the ways of thrifty self-discipline. Then there's the happy union of Ceÿx and Alcyone in book 11, so tragically shattered when Ceÿx drowns at sea in a storm. Disguised as Ceÿx, Morpheus, the god of sleep, appears to Alcyone in a dream and reveals the death. Alcyone throws herself into the sea in grief, only for the gods to take pity on her and Ceÿx by turning them both into kingfishers. Elsewhere in the mythological tradition they had earned the gods' wrath by hubristically calling each other Zeus and Hera, but Ovid omits this strand of their story. This omission is so conspicuous in Ovid's version that the silence significantly amplifies their goodness in book 11.

We've already seen in chapter 1 that a virtue much heralded by Augustus was *pietas*, or dutiful respect for the gods, country, and family. The likes of Philemon and Baucis well exemplify such religious *pietas* (8.631). As for filial *pietas*, Aeneas models it (13.626), thereby living up to his own self in the *Aeneid*. But another good example of its sacrosanct nature comes early in book 8, when King Minos of Crete lays siege to the Greek city of Megara. Scylla, daughter of King Nisus of Megara, falls in love with Minos and decides to betray her city to him. Minos has everything to gain, but he recoils with horror when Scylla makes her offer. "You blot on our age!" he cries; "I pray that the gods will banish you far / from their own bright sphere" (8.97–98). Given their waywardness thus far in the poem, Minos's faith in the gods' righteous indignation appears high-minded but naïve, as if this "just lawgiver" (8.101–2) is out of step with the real way of the world in the *Metamorphoses*.

These and many more examples of human dignity and commitment to principle show up the gods, then; and the gods regularly fail to show up to punish egregious human transgressors. Philomela and Procne set a trend by taking matters into their own hands. Other formidable female punishers soon emerge to dispense improvised justice. As we've seen in chapter 1, Pelias is punished in book 7 when Medea persuades his daughters inadvertently to kill him. In book 8, two of Althaea's brothers are killed by Meleäger, her son; he pays the penalty when, after an agonizing operetta of indecision, his mother finally decides to avenge her brothers by doing Meleäger to death. But for a closer look at one last example of a mortal taking matters into her own hands, let's fast-forward to the Trojan queen Hecuba in book 13.

Polydorus, Hecuba's youngest son, had been entrusted to Polymestor, king of Thrace, to keep him out of harm's way during the Trojan War. Polymestor lusts after the riches that come with Polydorus, and he promptly murders the boy, then hurling the corpse into the sea. Hecuba chances to find the mutilated body cast up on a beach. Just as Procne is shocked into silence when she decodes Philomela's tapestry, so Hecuba is rendered voiceless by the shock of discovery:

> Her attendants screamed, but the queen was totally dumb
>    in her anguish.
> Her voice was stifled.
> . . . . . . . . . . . . . . . . . . . . . . . . . . . .

> She stared at the ground directly before her, or else, with a
>     grim look,
> *lifted her eyes to the sky*, then gazed on her son as he lay there.
>
> (13.538–39, 541–42)

Why the detail of her lifting her eyes to the sky? If Hecuba is looking to the gods for their intervention, she looks in vain. Her anger bursts into an inferno of vengeful rage, but, as if a second Procne, her retribution is planned with cold precision. She meets with Polymestor and excites him with the prospect of yet more loot; but when he falsely swears that all the gold Hecuba gives him will go to Polydorus, she finally snaps. She gouges out Polymestor's eyes in an orgy of anger-fueled violence. Their king maimed, the Thracians pelt Hecuba with stones, and she snaps again, but this time as the snarling dog that she's suddenly become—the second time she loses her human voice in the episode.

Where are the gods in all this? After all that Hecuba has been through as a mother left bereft in the Trojan War, and after losing her daughter Polyxena as well as Polydorus in book 13, this is how the episode ends:

> Her Trojan friends and her Grecian foes were distressed
> alike by the fate of the queen; and all of the gods were
>     affected—
> every one of them. Even Jupiter's sister and consort
> declared that Hecuba hadn't deserved such an ending as that!
>
> (13.572–75)

A poignant conclusion to a distressing tragedy, but the gods' reaction here is too little too late. This after-the-event show of unanimity merely underscores their complete absence when Hecuba was going it alone, taking matters into her own hands because that was the only way in which justice would be served. And so when we revisit line 542 and find her lifting her eyes to the sky, we can now perhaps better infer her look: doesn't she send a vexed question mark heavenward? It's left to us to wonder if the gods were just casually indifferent to the human tragedy unfolding in Polydorus's case or—still worse—callously unmoved by it.

## Webs of Intrigue: Arachne Versus Minerva

So much for divine inaction in matters of crime and punishment in the *Metamorphoses*. Now for the problems that arise when they do take action, sometimes because mortal hubris demands it, but often high-handedly, occasionally out of whimsy or pique, and rarely with a judicious and reassuring sense of proportion. In turn, these divine actions have a direct bearing on the poem's political messaging: if Ovid's gods appear maverick and inconsistent in their adjudication of mortals, can Augustus avoid coming under suspicion because of his own divine credentials? Do we suspect that he resembles Ovid's Jove or that he's truer to the "real" Jupiter in his steady, august majesty? Is he just like the Ovidian Jove or righteous and just, like the Jove we hope for?

Let's first address certain extremes of behavior on the part of both gods and mortals as a preface of sorts to the ambiguities that complicate our star attraction in this section: the story of the wonder weaver Arachne's transformation into a spider at the start of book 6. First, a nasty case of divine spite. "The gods can feel anger [*ira*] too" (8.279): this much in the way of theological rumination before Ovid explains how Diana was offended at the Calydonian king Oeneus's failure to include her in his pious honoring of the gods. The omission may have been an accident ("Diana alone was forgotten," 8.277), but she hardly sees it that way. She unleashes a gigantic boar to plague Oeneus's kingdom, and much of book 8 is spent on recounting the epic story of how that scourge was at last destroyed. The massive beast appears almost as large as Diana's ego: this isn't the first time that she's reacted to a perceived slight with vast overkill, as we'll see in the case of Actaeon later in this chapter; but for now she usefully models the outer limits of divine intolerance in the *Metamorphoses*.

Second, notable cases of mortal hubris punished by the gods. In book 3, Pentheus, the king of Thebes "who treated the gods with contempt" (514), gets his comeuppance when he's no match for Bacchus and eventually torn to pieces by his own mother, the Bacchante Agave. Then, in book 6, the arrogant Niobe has pretensions to being treated like a goddess ("My beauty . . . is surely divine" [181]). Blessed with fourteen children, she outrages the goddess Latona by declaring war in the fertility stakes: she calls Latona, the mother of two children (Apollo and Diana), relatively childless by comparison with herself; but she pays for her hubris when all fourteen of her children are murdered, after which she's turned into a perpetually weeping rock. At the end of book 8, Erysichthon, that hater of the gods, desecrates the grove of Ceres by cutting down a sacred oak. The penalty for his impiety is to be wracked by insatiable hunger until he ends up cannibalizing himself, literally eating the hand that feeds himself; Ceres, the goddess of fertility and agriculture (hence "cereal" from her name), supplies enough for all the world bar him. Does the punishment fit the crime in these three cases of hubris, or do Bacchus, Latona, and Ceres go too far in their reprisals? Do they show the same strain of divine overkill that was glimpsed as early as book 1, in Jupiter's punishment of the entire human race for the wickedness of Lycaön alone? Ovid leaves such questions open, but the basic fact of asking-for-trouble hubris in Pentheus, etc., is surely incontestable.

These are extreme cases, certainly, but they usefully illuminate by contrast the ambivalences of a rather more nuanced case such as Arachne's. Minerva, patroness of spinning and weaving, hears that a certain Lydian girl, Arachne, claims to be her equal in working the wool. The goddess visits Arachne in disguise as a feeble old woman and urges her to show some modesty and "humbly crave [Minerva's] forgiveness / for boasting so rashly. The goddess will surely forgive if you ask her" (6.32–33). Arachne reacts angrily, rejecting the old woman's advice out of hand. Minerva reveals herself, Arachne refuses to back down, she challenges the goddess to a contest, and the two face off at their respective looms, both of them working at warp speed.

So far in the story matters are finely balanced: on the one side, Arachne is arrogant in her brash confidence, stubbornly intransigent, and downright rude; on the other side, Minerva is condescendingly superior, self-righteous, and thin-skinned. We're shown the tapestries that both simultaneously produce. Minerva's amounts to a sort of woolen Windsor Castle, highly controlled and formal in its spatial organization and with an imposing depiction of the Royal Family in full regalia: "The twelve Olympians, Jove in their midst, with august dignity / sat upon lofty thrones" (72–73). The main storyline that she weaves into her picture tells how she, Minerva/Athena, gained control of Athens and gave it her name: Neptune tried to compete with Minerva over the city, and he's shown in all his might on the tapestry, but he's no match for the triumphant Minerva ("The gods looked on in amazement, and victory crowned her endeavour" [82]). Be warned, Arachne! To press the point, Minerva adds four small representations, one in each corner (she's good at sharp elbows), of mortal women rashly competing against the gods; in each case they're punished with metamorphosis. The whole production is didactic in thrust, moral in force, and ominous in its show of divine power. It has "a border of olive branches, / symbol of peace" (101–2): a diplomatic touch, perhaps, but the air of menace remains, like the image of a dove engraved on a dagger's handle.

But then the gods cut loose: Arachne's tapestry is far less disciplined in the free-flowing movement of its images, and the gods themselves are far less disciplined in what they get up to in the twenty or so scenes that crowd the picture. The first scene portrays Europa being abducted by Jupiter in the guise of a bull, and it sets the tone for what's to come: the gods are shown at their very worst as first Jupiter and then Neptune and Apollo and Bacchus and Saturn (on and on!) commit rape after rape in a medley of metamorphic disguises and nasty deceptions. The passage is packed, dense, and highly allusive, as if Arachne's dossier of incriminating evidence is so vast that she can only fleetingly touch on the endless individual cases. In the language of Roman poetics, Minerva's tapestry is epic in its formal grandeur and in its "high" style and tenor; but Arachne's is nimbler in its quick and quirky movement from one scene to the next, and in referring to one arcane name or storyline after another, she evidently assumes that her reader-viewers know Robert Graves's *The Greek Myths* inside out. The gods may be disguised, but Arachne's skill is such that they appear visually true: in the Europa scene, "the bull and the sea were convincingly real" (104); more generally, "all these scenes were given authentic settings, the persons / their natural likeness" (121–22). Beyond this visual realism, however, has Arachne exposed a more chilling reality? The tabloid truth is out: in contrast to the fantasy image of divine decorum that Minerva projects, Arachne reveals what the likes of Jupiter are *really* like.

It's unclear in Ovid's account whether Arachne actually looks at, or deigns to look at, Minerva's tapestry. If we infer not, it may be a sign of Arachne's self-absorption and arrogant disdain; or maybe she doesn't look because the virginal Minerva is so wedded to the Firm, so prudish and by the book, that her picture's conservative content is all too predictable. But when Minerva sees Arachne's tapestry, this is what happens:

> Not Pallas [= Minerva], not even the goddess of Envy
>     could criticize weaving
> like that. The fair-haired warrior goddess resented
>     Arachne's
> success and ripped up the picture betraying the gods'
>     misdemeanours.
>
> (6.129–31)

After ripping up Arachne's picture, Minerva uses her boxwood shuttle to assault her. Arachne tries to hang herself, only for the goddess to take pity and save her; but Arachne is still punished for her presumption when Minerva turns her into a web-weaving spider. Where to start with the ambiguities raised by these developments? What precisely does Arachne's "success" (131) consist in? Her consummate skill, the unerring accuracy of her tell-all exposé of the gods, or a combination of both? What causes Minerva to react to Arachne's tapestry with such anger and violence: personal jealousy at the upstart's divine abilities or Establishment outrage at such a dissing of divine authority? As for Arachne, she's partly the persecuted victim of her sublime talent but partly also the victim of her insufferable arrogance. Minerva gave her a chance to back down before the contest. It was Arachne who willfully called that contest, and even though Minerva resorts to violence after the contest, she then reverts to pity. Do these points count for nothing in Minerva's favor?

A balanced perspective is needed, and Ovid supplies it. This is how he describes the imperceptibly merging colorations of the threads on the looms of both Minerva and Arachne:

> Think how a tract of the sky, when the sun breaks suddenly
> through
> at the end of a rain shower, is steeped in the long, great
> curve of a rainbow;
> the bow is agleam with a range of a thousand various hues,
> but the eye cannot tell where one fades into another; adjacent
> tones are so much the same, though the difference is clear
> at the edges.
> Such were the colours the two contestants used in the fabric.
>
> (6.63–68)

The rainbow analogy is symbolically suggestive on a number of levels. Like colors that are starkly different at the outer edges of the rainbow's bands, Arachne and Minerva, god and mortal (and lowly mortal at that!), are wholly dissimilar in status, privilege, and world outlook. But like the colors merging seamlessly together at their meeting point, the two weavers can't be told apart in their shared skill at the loom. Their representations of the gods couldn't be more different. Jupiter is so dignified and august on the one hand (Minerva) but so predatory and sex-mad on the other (Arachne): here are completely incompatible colorations of the same god, yet they touch and merge in the totality of the two tapestries, just as they do in the paradox of Jupiter's larger characterization in the *Metamorphoses*. He's King of the Gods, but he's also king of the swingers. He's supremely powerful yet supremely sordid. Only a seamless merging of the two weavings would accurately capture the "true" Jove of the *Metamorphoses*—and the "true" Neptune, the "true" Apollo, etc.

No wonder the workings of divine justice in such a world are so inconsistent and inscrutable: what version of Jupiter (or of any other of the gods) is going to show up on any given day or in any given episode—the Minerva model, Arachne's type, or something in between? On this approach, the Minerva-Arachne sequence offers a really telling insight into how Ovid's divine machinery operates in the poem more generally. He clearly saw special creative opportunity in the myth: we can infer as much partly from the fact that Arachne's story is unprecedented earlier in the extant Greco-Roman literary tradition apart from an oblique reference in Virgil's *Georgics*, and that no obvious models appear to have shaped his treatment. But another draw was its Augustan implications. Remember that moment when, on Minerva's tapestry, Jupiter and the Olympians are shown sitting on their thrones "with august dignity," *augusta gravitate* in the Latin (6.73)? The echo of Augustus's name here is unmistakable, and perhaps intimidatingly so. Arachne pushes back powerfully against the official portrait of the gods that Minerva propagates, bravely exposing the complacent hypocrisy underlying that authorized version. Can we exempt Augustus from the web of intrigue that Arachne weaves? Through her, we suspect, Ovid puts a spidery finger on the problem of reconciling image and reality—the face of power, and how it really works—in Augustus's Rome.

## Actaeon, Ovid's Mistake, and the Wages of Error

But what about wrongdoings committed in error? How to judge them, and to what extent should the wrongdoer be held accountable for such misdemeanors? Harmful mistakes committed in ignorance and/or by accident abound throughout the *Metamorphoses*, and in all sorts of contexts. In book 7, for example, the complicated love story of Cephalus and Procris ends in tragedy when Cephalus accidently kills his wife with the never-erring javelin that she'd given him as a gift. An avid hunter, he calls to the breeze (*aura* in the Latin, a feminine noun) to cool him down in the midday heat. Procris hears a rumor that Cephalus has been serenading a lover called *Aura*, and so she follows him to his hunting grounds. She hides in the brush; he hears a rustling and thinks it's an animal. He shoots, she dies, and both are mistaken, she about *aura/Aura*, he about his target—a tragedy that turns on "the confusion of a name," *errorem . . . nominis* in the Latin (7.857).

We could linger on many more stories of disastrous error in the *Metamorphoses*, but what matters for now is the word *error* itself. Ovid's use of it in the Cephalus story at the end of book 7 is suggestive: its thematic centrality to many episodes is symbolized by this occurrence of the term roughly at the poem's midpoint. Surely its most notorious occurrence comes in Ovid's treatment of Actaeon in book 3—a story we've already touched on in chapter 1, but let's now consider it in a bit more detail.

Actaeon, a young Theban prince, is devoted to hunting, but he becomes the hunted after incurring the wrath of Diana. He leads his comrades on the morning chase, and their haul is good before the noonday sun begins to take its toll and they stop for a rest. Actaeon goes off on his own, "saunter[ing] aimlessly through the unfamiliar woodland" (175, where the Latin for "sauntering" is *errans*, from the verb that's cognate to the noun *error*). Wandering into a clearing, he stumbles upon the goddess as she bathes with her attendant nymphs in a spring. Though the nymphs try to screen her, "her neck and shoulders were visible over the heads of her maidens" (182). Livid at being seen naked even to this extent, and to ensure that he remains silent about what he's witnessed, Diana transforms Actaeon into a stag that is then tortured by the loss of his human voice: yet another punitive silencing in the *Metamorphoses*! His own hunting dogs catch sight of the stag: they relentlessly track him down, unaware that he's their beloved master, and he's powerless to call off the very hounds that are devoted to him. He's torn to bits, and "only after his life was destroyed in a welter of wounds / is Diana . . . said to have cooled her anger" (251–52).

How to judge this case? Ovid explicitly introduces Actaeon's misdemeanor as an innocent error:

> If you look at the facts, however, you'll find that chance
> was the culprit.
> No crime was committed. Why punish a man for a pure
> mistake [*error*]?
>
> (3.141–42)

But after Actaeon's death, opinion is more divided:

> Comments varied: some felt that the goddess had overdone
> her violent revenge, while others commended it—worthy,
> they said,
> of her strict virginity. All were prepared to defend their
> opinion.
>
> (3.253–55)

It's as if Ovid steps outside the poem in lines 141–42 and weighs Actaeon's case from a detached, external viewpoint: when you approach the matter from that measured perspective, how can Actaeon's innocent error be interpreted as a crime in the first place, let alone one deserving to be so harshly punished? But the reactions registered in lines 253–55 are much more internal to the world of the *Metamorphoses*, as if informed by the respondents' experience of just how divine justice really works in this poetic universe. Some felt Diana had overdone it: a judgment solely on the specific case, or one shaped by context? Diana already has form in the poem: we saw earlier how she turns nastily on Callisto in book 2 after the nymph had been raped and impregnated by Jupiter, and her nasty streak is frequently visible later in the work. Is it any surprise that Diana overdid it in Actaeon's case? And can't we now recast lines 253–54 to the effect of: "some felt that the goddess had *of course*, and *very predictably*, overdone her violent revenge"? As for those who commended it as "worthy of Diana's strict virginity," such highness of principle is all very well. But where's the outrage when mortal virginity is endangered and/or stolen by the gods in the cases of Daphne, Syrinx, and Io in book 1 alone? And the absence of any margin for mortal error surely fits well enough with the kneejerk recourse to punishment that the gods regularly dish out in the *Metamorphoses* in reaction to the pettiest slights, real or perceived.

If we're inclined to view Actaeon as the blameless victim of divine pique, his case, extreme though it is, well captures the inconsistent and often disproportionate nature of divine justice more generally in the *Metamorphoses*. What, then, of justice as administered by Augustus, that Jupiter on earth? Let's now turn to the second book of Ovid's exilic *Tristia*, which is cast in the form of an elegiac letter to Augustus. In it, Ovid addresses the two reasons that led the emperor to banish him, "a poem and a blunder" (*carmen et error* [2.207]). As we saw in the introduction, the poem is the risqué *Art of Love*: much of Ovid's address to Augustus in *Tristia* 2 is a defense of it against the charge of immorality. As for Ovid's mysterious blunder, many theories of what happened have been proposed, some of them plausible, most of them improbable (to say the least), none compelling. Unless some new evidence were magically to come to light, the truth about Ovid's mistake is now surely beyond recovery. But whatever that elusive reality, far more important for present purposes is how, in his letter to Augustus, he articulates his *error* in terms of Actaeon's fate.

This is how Ovid describes his blunder:

> Why did I see anything? Why did I make my eyes guilty?
> Why was I so thoughtless as to harbour the knowledge of
>     a fault?
> Unwitting was Actaeon when he beheld Diana unclothed;
> none the less he became the prey of his own hounds.
> Clearly, among the gods, even ill-fortune must be
>     atoned for,
> nor is mischance an excuse when a deity is wronged.
> On that day when my ruinous mistake [*error*] ravished
>     me away,
> my house, humble but stainless, was destroyed.
>
> (*Tristia* 2.103–10; trans. A. L. Wheeler)

We saw in chapter 2 how Ovid's praises of Julius Caesar late in *Metamorphoses* 15 are potentially compromised by an ambivalence in the word *scilicet*: *of course* Caesar's greatest achievement was his fathering of Augustus—a self-evident fact, or an obvious absurdity? So with the word for "clearly," *scilicet*, in line 107. *Clearly* the gods regard accidental blunders as fully culpable and inexcusable: a fact of life to which Ovid meekly resigns himself, or an obvious absurdity that draws an ironic protest from him? But the Actaeon allusion suggests at least two things more. First, even though Ovid is talking primarily of his *error* here, Actaeon's metamorphosis into a stag, the loss of his human voice, and his fate at the jaws of his own dogs also offer a tempting analogy for the consequences of Ovid's *Art of Love*: the poet too has been punished with metamorphosis by an angry god; he too loses his voice both through the censorship of his writings at Rome and the dearth (he claims) of Latin speakers in his place of exile; and just as Actaeon is killed by his own dogs, so in his different way Ovid is figuratively destroyed by his own *Art of Love*.

Second, Ovid's circumspect description of his blunder via the Actaeon analogy is itself telling. His refusal fully to explain his *error* at any point in his exilic poetry generates an air of mystery that may partly be meant to keep us interested; he draws attention to the mystery precisely by saying so little about it. Might he suddenly decide to reveal all at any given moment, however embarrassing the revelations might be for himself . . . and for Augustus? Or does he recognize the dangers inherent in frankly confessing and explaining his mistake? If you make your confession but not to the level expected by those who control your fate, you're asking for further trouble; and if you abjectly admit your guilt in the hope of some concession in return, you're only playing into your punisher's hands. Better, surely, to say little or nothing that risks making your current plight worse.

Beyond these uncertainties, Ovid repeatedly insists on fine distinctions in describing his fateful mistake in his exilic writings: the *error* was an indiscretion and therefore blameworthy, a *culpa*, but apparently not a crime as such, a *crimen* or *scelus*, and not a sin, a *peccatum*, committed with forethought. As he sifts through the vocabulary of wrongdoing in this way, you get the sense that he's trying to articulate as precisely as he can an offense that's hard to pin down, as if it eludes easy terms of text-book legal definition; or that he struggles to understand what exactly it was in his innocent mistake that was apparently culpable enough to earn him such a harsh penalty. But all this legal nicety ultimately counts for nothing, and this is perhaps Ovid's sharper point: there's only one arbiter of his case who ultimately matters, and all this stress on subtle linguistic shading gets us nowhere when Augustus (we all know!) will unilaterally decide Ovid's fate once and for all, and solely on the emperor's terms.

The *error* lurks in Ovid's exilic poetry, then, as the Great Mystery that constantly causes us to scratch our heads: what on earth did he do to get himself banished to the ends of the earth? Ovid's lament that he "made his eyes guilty" has led to a good deal of fanciful speculation about what the compromising spectacle might have been. But couldn't Ovid be casting his *error* in the figurative language of "seeing something he shouldn't" as a prelude here to the Actaeon analogy that follows, as if fitting his blunder to suit the terms of the Actaeon story? Whatever the now-irrecoverable truth of the matter, the implication remains that Ovid, like Actaeon, has been disproportionately punished by a spiteful and vindictive divinity. And whatever else he may have witnessed of a compromising nature, Ovid too has seen a naked god, albeit only *after* his fateful mistake was made: he's seen the bare truth of what Augustan "justice" really looks like behind the façade of due process and clemency. "Mischance has no excuse [*veniam*] when a deity is wronged" (2.108): Ovid regularly uses the word *venia* in the exilic poetry and elsewhere of Augustus's reputation as a pardoner, but so much for that reputation in Ovid's own case.

But while the Actaeon of the *Metamorphoses* offers one important model for how Ovid articulates his *error* in his exilic phase and for how harshly it's been punished, other models also suggest themselves. It's striking that many artists come to a bad end in the *Metamorphoses*: prominent among them are the uppity daughters of Pierus in book 5 (defeated by the Muses in a singing contest and punished thereafter by transformation into raucous magpies) and Arachne and Marsyas in book 6. Artists such as these are cocky and confident, yes, and to a degree they deserve their comeuppance in their respective stories; but do they deserve to suffer quite as they do? Beyond the Actaeon analogy, we're left to ask what implications the fates of these artists might have for how we begin to think about Ovid's treatment at the hands of Augustus.

In his exilic poetry Ovid likens Augustus's banishment of him to being struck by Jupiter's bolt. So in the very first of his *Tristia*:

> I too admit—for I have felt it—that I fear the weapon of
> Jupiter:
> I believe myself the target of a hostile bolt whenever the
> thunder roars.
>
> (1.1.81–82; trans. A. L. Wheeler)

In playing the penitent in Tomis, Ovid tactfully—and tactically—acknowledges Augustus's relative restraint in *only* banishing him (it could have been worse . . .), and he keeps hoping for a reprieve from his sentence or at least some mitigation if it. But in light of what the gods of the *Metamorphoses* do to artists who challenge them and to poor unfortunates like Actaeon, the allusions to the Jovian bolt in Ovid's exilic writings instantly bristle with a lingering sense of menace even after his downfall.

Let's now imagine that Ovid revised the *Metamorphoses* in Tomis so as to align his own experience with that of persecuted artists like Arachne and Marsyas, and that he passes oblique judgment on the Augustan times by implicitly identifying himself with Actaeon. An attractive hypothesis, certainly, and one beneficially explored by modern scholars. But how to be sure, at this distance of time, that any such revisions or importations were made only after Ovid was exiled? For all its enticements, this hypothesis surely relies too much on what's too little known, and so let's consider an alternative possibility.

Whatever the exact nature of Ovid's blunder, the theme of *error* was no new fixation of his in the exilic poetry. It was already a major preoccupation in the *Metamorphoses* and central there to Ovid's portrayal of the vagaries of divine justice. His depictions of persecuted artists may uncannily anticipate his own punishment at the hands of Augustus in 8 CE, but that overlap need hardly be a fortuitous coincidence. The exilic poetry delivers on a storyline foretold in the *Metamorphoses*, as if now applying to Ovid himself the "code" of divine anger and vindictiveness that had already prevailed in his poem of change. Hence, perhaps, his deeper meaning when he explicitly refers to his exile in terms of the *Metamorphoses* at the end of *Tristia* 1.1 (Ovid is sending the personified book 1 of his *Tristia* from Tomis to Rome and warns it to be on the lookout for the *Metamorphoses* in his hearth and home there):

There are also thrice five rolls about changing forms,

poems recently saved from the burial of my fortunes.

To these I bid you say that the aspect of my own fate can

now be reckoned among those metamorphosed figures.

(1.1.117–20; trans. A. L. Wheeler)

The author of change himself becomes the face of change, and the *Metamorphoses* takes on a new relevance when viewed through the prism of the *Tristia*. To revisit "the wrath of Jupiter" (*Iovis ira*) that was our starting point in this chapter: Ovid's time-defying *Metamorphoses* will be immune to that *Iovis ira*, he tells us in the epilogue at the end of book 15, only for his fortunes to be suddenly transformed. In articulating his experience in terms of the *Metamorphoses*, the first book of his *Tristia* functions a bit like a book 16 addendum to his magnum opus. In that book 16 it's "Jupiter's wrath" that's the winner, and nothing has changed: Augustus's anger, we discover, follows the pattern of impenetrable divine *ira* that was set in the *Met.* Life imitates art with cruel irony when Ovid is consigned to his fate by the god-in-waiting he fêtes in *Metamorphoses* 15, and his personal story then travels on—and unravels—in *Met.* 16.

# Epilogue

J ust what do we mean when we say that a famous Greco-Roman text is still "relevant" in our twenty-first-century times? Many answers could of course be ventured. Plato and Aristotle, for obvious example, have cast a vast shadow over the history of Western philosophy down to the present day. Greek tragedy continues to be reconceived in performance on the modern stage, often to the effect of exploring lines of continuity and difference between ancient and modern forms of reflection on fundamental moral questions. In recent decades, the surge of interest in philosophy as a way of life has drawn a more popular audience to writers such as Seneca, Epictetus, and Marcus Aurelius in the first and second centuries CE—writers who apply their Stoic philosophy to negotiating the day-to-day pressures of life. It's little wonder that many suggestive precedents for techniques of cognitive-behavioral therapy have been found in ancient Stoicism or that the likes of Seneca are a familiar presence on the shelves of Barnes and Noble.

What, then, of Ovid's *Metamorphoses*? It's been massively influential in the history of Western art as well as literature, and the creative spark that it has provided for reflection on the nature and meaning of metamorphosis itself continues undimmed today: witness, for example, *After Ovid: New Metamorphoses*, the 1994 anthology of modern renderings edited by Michael Hofmann and James Lasdun; Ted Hughes's 1997 *Tales from Ovid*; Mary Zimmerman's Tony Award–winning adaption of the *Metamorphoses* that ran on Broadway from March 2002 to February 2003; or, most recently, the poet and dramatist Michael Symmons Roberts's radio series entitled *Modern Metamorphoses*, broadcast early in 2021 on BBC Radio 4—a series that traced the lineage of poetic treatments of metamorphosis from Homer and Ovid down to reimaginings of the *Metamorphoses* in our own times.

This book has focused not on the literary and artistic reception of the *Metamorphoses* but on the ways it can enrich and inform our own twenty-first-century lives by shedding light on a perennial question: how do we begin to make sense of the world about us, and of our place in that world, when change is encoded into our existence—when our identities are always evolving according to our circumstances at any given life moment, the company we keep, the sociocultural influences that shape our existence, our opportunities (economic, educational, political, etc.) for growth and advancement in life, our emotional needs and commitments, and so on? It's of course important to proceed cautiously: quite apart from the need for a balanced perspective (for most of us the changefulness of life is ever in tension with the unchanging steadiness, even the drudgery, of daily routines), any attempt to find in the *Metamorphoses* contact points with, or provocations to reflect on, many aspects of our own lived experience in the 2020s can't just ignore the historical factors that conditioned Ovid's writing in his own time. Hence our approach to the poem in these pages has been grounded in the sociocultural realities of the age of Augustus, and we've explored the political context in which Ovid wrote the *Metamorphoses* before his exile to Tomis in 8 CE.

But beyond the duties of historical contextualization, and despite our remote distance from Ovid's Rome, the more human side of the poem allows certain leaps of the imagination to be attempted from his times to our own. For all its portrayals of physical cruelty, rape, deception, and divine callousness, the *Metamorphoses* remains a precious resource that we can use and learn from today: such has been the thrust of this little book, and the aim has been to be merely suggestive, and certainly not prescriptive, about what we can take from the poem. In that spirit, let's briefly hazard three last impressions.

First, we've seen that the *Metamorphoses* offers a vision of changefulness that was in tension with Augustus's effort to restabilize Rome after the ravaging effects of long-term civil discord in the first-century BCE. It's important to recognize what's lost when the poem is read out of its historical context: much of its contemporary meaning in Augustus's Rome can too easily pass unrecognized. But a certain freedom from that historical frame also allows us to take ownership of the poem for ourselves, to personalize our reading of it, and to view our own life experiences in light of those that Ovid features across the fifteen books: growing to maturity, say, or finding our "true" selves, exploring our sexuality, coming to terms with aging and bereavement, calling out our oppressors, and learning to listen for what someone's really saying behind the façade of words. Many more aspects of this human face of the poem could be cited here, but the stimulus to comparison is all: we read ourselves by reading the *Metamorphoses*.

Second, and to develop this last point: the challenge to self-examination that Ovid offers is hardly exclusive to him, of course; even if the forms of examination may differ, much the same could be said of Shakespeare, say, or Dostoevsky, Jane Austen or Toni Morrison. Immediately striking, however, is the sheer intensity of the focus and alertness that Ovid requires of us in responding to his Latin—his exquisite control of tone, nuance, implication, and subtext. Even if his finer meanings are often lost in translation, a similar intensity of concentration is needed when we read him in English. Further, many of his stories in the *Metamorphoses* have a surface charm and simplicity to them that belie their literary complexity, their subtle allusions to many underlying sources, and the lurking ironies that are so often encased in Ovid's language. You can't read the *Metamorphoses* passively, and the challenge is to try to meet Ovid at least halfway—to be activated by reading him, to be alive to his sleight of hand and lightness of touch, and to recognize that the poem is an interactive construct that *requires* our fully engaged participation. If we allow ourselves to become Ovid's passengers, we are only half-readers.

Third, and finally: Ovid himself gives us encouragement to view our own lived experience in relation to the countless human dramas of change that are played out in the *Metamorphoses*. In his exilic writings, we remember (chapter 4), he explicitly casts the poem as an *imago*, a reflection, of his own transformed circumstances after his banishment to Tomis. At the end of chapter 4, we also considered the possibility that our poet in exile casts his fate at the hands of Augustus as akin to that of artists in the *Metamorphoses* such as Arachne and Marsyas—artists harshly punished by the gods they rashly challenge in contests of skill. Ovid read his own life experience through the prism of his poem of change. The twenty-first-century reader may of course find a very different point or form of empathetic engagement with the *Metamorphoses*, but what matters is the interactive impulse in the first place: we follow Ovid's example by reading with an eye on ourselves. So it is that Ovid himself models an approach to the poem that would doubtless have appealed to Narcissus.

# Further Reading

There is a vast modern bibliography on Ovid, and only a few suggestions can be made here.

## Overviews of Ovid's Life and Poetic Career

Fulkerson, Laurel. *Ovid: A Poet on the Margins*. London: Bloomsbury Academic, 2016.

Holzberg, Niklas. *Ovid: The Poet and His Work*. Ithaca, NY: Cornell University Press, 2002.

Mack, Sara. *Ovid*. New Haven, CT: Yale University Press, 1988.

Morgan, Llewelyn. *Ovid: A Very Short Introduction*. Oxford: Oxford University Press, 2020.

Newlands, Carole E. *Ovid*. Understanding Classics. London: I. B. Tauris, 2015.

Volk, Katharina. *Ovid*. Blackwell Introductions to the Classical World. Malden, MA: Wiley-Blackwell, 2010.

## Companions to Ovid

Boyd, Barbara W., ed. *Brill's Companion to Ovid*. Leiden: Brill, 2002.

Hardie, Philip, ed. *The Cambridge Companion to Ovid*. Cambridge: Cambridge University Press, 2002.

Knox, Peter E., ed. *A Companion to Ovid.* Blackwell Companions to the Ancient World. Malden, MA: Wiley-Blackwell, 2009.

## Specifically on the *Metamorphoses*

Fantham, Elaine. *Ovid's "Metamorphoses."* Oxford Approaches to Classical Literature. Oxford: Oxford University Press, 2004.

Liveley, Genevieve. *Ovid's "Metamorphoses": A Reader's Guide.* London: Continuum, 2011.

## Gender and Sexuality in the *Metamorphoses*

Lateiner, Donald. "Transsexuals and Transvestites in Ovid's *Metamorphoses.*" In *Bodies and Boundaries in Graeco-Roman Antiquity*, ed. T. Fögen and M. M. Lee, 125–54. Berlin: Walter de Gruyter, 2009.

Ormand, Kirk. "Impossible Lesbians in Ovid's *Metamorphoses.*" In *Gendered Dynamics in Latin Love Poetry*, ed. R. Ancona and E. Greene, 79–110. Baltimore, MD: Johns Hopkins University Press, 2005.

Salzman-Mitchell, Patricia. *A Web of Fantasies: Gaze, Image, and Gender in Ovid's "Metamorphoses."* Columbus: Ohio State University Press, 2005.

Sharrock, Alison. "Womanufacture." *Journal of Roman Studies* 81 (1991): 36–49.

## On the Reception of the *Metamorphoses*

Barkan, Leonard. *The Gods Made Flesh: Metamorphosis and the Pursuit of Paganism.* New Haven, CT: Yale University Press, 1986.

Brown, Sarah A. *Ovid: Myth and Metamorphosis.* Ancients in Action. London: Bristol Classical Press, 2005.

Enenkel, K. A. E., and J. L. de Jong, eds. *Re-inventing Ovid's "Metamorphoses": Pictorial and Literary Transformations in Various Media, 1400–1800*. Intersections 70. Leiden: Brill, 2020.

Lyne, Raphael. *Ovid's Changing Worlds: English "Metamorphoses," 1567–1632*. Oxford: Oxford University Press, 2001.

Martindale, Charles, ed. *Ovid Renewed: Ovidian Influences on Literature and Art from the Middle Ages to the Twentieth Century*. Cambridge: Cambridge University Press, 1988.

Miller, J. F., and C. E. Newlands, eds. *The Wiley-Blackwell Handbook to the Reception of Ovid*. Malden, MA: Wiley-Blackwell, 2014.

## Ovid as Butterfly

Tabucchi, Antonio. *Sogni di sogni*. Palermo: Sellerio Editore, 1992. (The second *Sogno* features Ovid's dream that, newly beloved by Augustus, he returns to Rome from exile in Tomis; he returns in the form of a giant butterfly that ends up de-winged, disfigured, and death-bound, Augustus's victim once more.)

## On Ovid's Environmental Imagination

Martelli, Francesca K. A. *Ovid*. Leiden: Brill, 2020.

Sissa, Giulia. "Apples and Poplars, Nuts and Bulls: The Poetic Biosphere of Ovid's *Metamorphoses*." In *Antiquities Beyond Humanism*, ed. E. Bianchi, S. Brill, and B. Holmes, 159–85. Oxford: Oxford University Press, 2019.

## Pedagogical Approaches

Boyd, B. W., and C. Fox, eds. *Approaches to Teaching the Works of Ovid and the Ovidian Tradition*. MLA Approaches to Teaching World Literature 113. New York: Modern Language Association of America, 2010.

Gloyn, Elizabeth. "Reading Rape in Ovid's *Metamorphoses*: A Test-Case Lesson." *Classical World* 106, no. 4 (2013): 676–81.

Newlands, Carole E. "Select Ovid." *Classical World* 102, no. 2 (2009): 173–77.

## Selected Studies

Curran, Leo C. "Rape and Rape-Victims in the *Metamorphoses*." *Arethusa* 11 (1978): 213–41.

Feeney, Denis C. *The Gods in Epic: Poetics and Critics of the Classical Tradition*. Oxford: Oxford University Press, 1991.

Feldherr, Andrew. *Playing Gods: Ovid's "Metamorphoses" and the Politics of Fiction*. Princeton, NJ: Princeton University Press, 2010.

Fulkerson, L., and T. Stover, eds. *Repeat Performances: Ovidian Repetition and the "Metamorphoses."* Madison: University of Wisconsin Press, 2016.

Galinsky, G. Karl. *Ovid's "Metamorphoses": An Introduction to the Basic Aspects*. Berkeley: University of California Press, 1975.

Hardie, Philip. *Ovid's Poetics of Illusion*. Cambridge: Cambridge University Press, 2002.

Hardie, Philip, A. Barchiesi, and S. E. Hinds, eds. *Ovidian Transformations: Essays on Ovid's "Metamorphoses" and Its Reception*. Cambridge Philological Society Supplement 23. Cambridge: Cambridge Philological Society, 1999.

James, Sharon L. "Rape and Repetition in Ovid's *Metamorphoses*: Myth, History, Structure, Rome." In *Repeat Performances: Ovidian Repetition and the "Metamorphoses,"* ed. L. Fulkerson and T. Stover, 154–75. Madison: University of Wisconsin Press, 2016.

Johnson, Patricia J. *Ovid Before Exile: Art and Punishment in the "Metamorphoses."* Madison: University of Wisconsin Press, 2008.

Keith, Alison M. *The Play of Fictions: Studies in Ovid's "Metamorphoses" Book 2*. Ann Arbor: University of Michigan Press, 1992.

Myers, K. Sara. *Ovid's Causes: Cosmogony and Aetiology in the "Metamorphoses."* Ann Arbor: University of Michigan Press, 1994.

Nagle, Betty R. "Byblis and Myrrha: Two Incest Narratives in the *Metamorphoses*." *Classical Journal* 78 (1983): 301–15.

Newlands, Carole E. "Violence and Resistance in Ovid's *Metamorphoses*." In *Texts and Violence in the Roman World*, ed. M. R. Gale and J. H. D. Scourfield, 140–78. Cambridge: Cambridge University Press, 2018.

Pavlock, Barbara. *The Image of the Poet in Ovid's "Metamorphoses."* Madison: University of Wisconsin Press, 2009.

Richlin, Amy. "Reading Ovid's Rapes." In *Arguments with Silence: Writing the History of Roman Women*, 130–65. Ann Arbor: University of Michigan Press, 2014.

Sharrock, A., D. Möller, and M. Malm, eds. *Metamorphic Readings: Transformation, Language, and Gender in the Interpretation of Ovid's "Metamorphoses."* Oxford: Oxford University Press, 2020.

Solodow, Joseph B. *The World of Ovid's "Metamorphoses."* Chapel Hill: University of North Carolina Press, 1988.

Tissol, Garth. *The Face of Nature: Wit, Narrative, and Cosmic Origins in Ovid's "Metamorphoses."* Princeton, NJ: Princeton University Press, 1997.

Wheeler, Stephen M. *A Discourse of Wonders: Audience and Performance in Ovid's "Metamorphoses."* Philadelphia: University of Pennsylvania Press, 1999.

# Index